DICTIONARY OF SPECIAL EDUCATION

DICTIONARY OF SPECIAL EDUCATION

Dr. Seema Singh, Reader
Faculty of Education
B.H.U.
Varanasi (U.P.)

KANISHKA PUBLISHERS, DISTRIBUTORS
NEW DELHI-110 002

KANISHKA PUBLISHERS, DISTRIBUTORS
4697/5-21A, Ansari Road, Daryaganj
New Delhi -110 002
Phones : 2327 0497, 232 8 8285
Fax : 011-2328 8285
E-mail : kanishka_publishing@yahoo.co.in
kanishkabooks@gmail.com

Dictionary of Special Education

First Published-2007

Edition-2023

ISBN : 978-81-7391-904-6

PRINTED IN INDIA

Published by Madan Sachdeva for Kanishka Publishers, Distributors, 4697/5-21A, Ansari Road, Daryaganj, New Delhi-110002, Typeset by Sunshine Graphics, Delhi, and Printed at G.S. Printers, Delhi.

Dedicated
to
My Mother Dr. Kusum Singh
and
Daughter Ashi

Preface

Every tenth person in the world is estimated to be inflicted with one or the other kind of disability. The person with disabilities needs physical, educational, social and emotional rehabilitation. Education plays an important role in all-round development of children. Special education deals with the education of children with special needs (handicapped) in all settings including special schools, integrated and inclusive settings or non-formal education. Trained manpower is required to cater to the needs of different disabilities. With the enactment of RCI Act 1992 and PWD Act 1995, education and rehabilitation of handicapped are gaining momentum in India.

The idea of compiling the dictionary of special education came due to the dearth of books where concept of words related with special education are explained in simple manner. In this dictionary, the words have been carefully selected, edited, compiled and arranged in alphabetical order. The words are chosen and selected from disciplines such as general psychology, education, social psychology, abnormal psychology, physiology etc. The words are explained with special reference to handicapped children. This dictionary will be of immense value to the students in the field of special education.

I am thankful to Mr. A. Thanudurai for typing the drafts of manuscript. I will be failing in my duties if I do not place on record my sincere appreciation for the job done and mental support given by my husband Mr. U.K. Singh, son Ansh and younger brother Rohit Kr. Singh. I cannot forget to remember my father late Shri R.R. Singh and mother late Dr. Kusum Singh who always encouraged me during their lifetime.

I will appreciate and acknowledge suggestions and comments from my readers for improvement of this dictionary.

Dr. Seema Singh

Abbreviations

AAMR	American Association on Mental Retardation
ABR	Auditory Brainstem Response
ADA	Americans with Disabilities Act A Civil Rights Law passed in 1990 that does not allow discrimination against people with disabilities in employment, public service and public accommodations
ADD	Attention Deficit Disorder
ADHD	Attention Deficit Hyperactive Disorder
AD	Alerting Devices
ADL	Activities of Daily Living
AFB	American Foundation for the Blind
ALD	Assistive Learning Devices
ALIMCO	Artificial Limb Manufacturing Corporation of India
AMA	American Medical Association
APA	American Psychological Association
ASHA	American Speech & Hearing Association
ASL	American Sign Language (Sign language for deaf adults in North America. It has its own grammar)
AT	Assistive Technology
AUSLAN	Australian Sign Language
AYJNIHH	Ali Yavar Jung National Institute for Hearing Handicapped
BERA	Brainstem Evoked Response Audiometry
BIP	Behavioral Intervention Plan
BLAT	Blind Learning Aptitude Test
BSL	British Sign Language
CBR	Community Based Rehabilitation
CEC	Council of Exceptional Children

CIET	Central Institute of Educational Technology
CMR	Custodial Mentally Retarded
DB	Deaf Blindness
DD	Developmental Delay
DIAL	Developmental Indicator for the Assessment of Learning Disabilities
DIET	District Institute of Education and Training
DPEP	District Primary Education Programme
ECHCA	Education for All Handicapped Children Act (Passed in 1975, United States)
ECSE	Early Childhood Special Education
ECT	Electro Convulsive Therapy
ED	Emotional Disturbance
EEG	Electro Encephalogram
EFA	Education For All
EHA	Education for All Handicapped Act
EMR	Educable Mentally Retarded
FAS	Fetal Alcohol Syndrome
HI	Hearing Impairment
ICDS	Integrated Child Development Services
IDEA	Individuals with Disabilities Education Act
IED	Integrated Education for the Disabled
IEDC	Integrated Education for Disabled Children
IEP	Individualized Educational Programme
IFSP	Individualized Family Service Plan
IMA	Indian Manual Alphabet
IPH	The Institute for the Physically Handicapped
ISL	Indian Sign Language
ISS	Indian Sign System
ITPA	Illinois Test of Psycholinguistic Abilities
IYDP	International Year of Disabled Persons
LD	Learning Disability
LRE	Least Restrictive Environment
MBD	Minimal Brain Dysfunction
MD	Multiple Disabilities

MDT	Multi Disciplinary Evaluation
MHRD	Ministry of Human Resource and Development
MLL	Minimum Level of Learning
MR	Mental Retardation
MRI	Magnetic Resonance Imaging
MSJE	Ministry of Social Justice & Empowerment
NCERT	National Council for Educational Research & Training
NCTE	National Council for Teacher Education
NGO	Non-Government Organization
NHFDC	National Handicapped Finance and Development Corporation
NICDR	National Information Centre on Disabled & Rehabilitation
NIMH	National Institute of Mentally Handicapped
NIOH	National Institute of Orthopaedically Handicapped
NIRTAR	National Institute for Rehabilitation, Training and Research
NIVH	National Institute for Visually Handicapped
NJCLD	National Joint Committee on Learning Disabilities
NOS	National Open School
NPRPD	National Programme for Rehabilitation of Persons with Disabilities
NPE	National Policy on Education
NTA	National Trust Act
OHI	Other Health Impairment
OI	Orthopaedic Impairment
OM	Orientation & Mobility Services
OT	Occupational Therapy
PIED	Project Integrated Education for the Disabled
PMR	Profound Mentally Retarded
POA	Programme of Action
PT	Physical Therapy
PWD	Persons with Disability Act
SCERT	State Council for Educational Research and Training

SD	Severe Disability
SE	Special Education
SLD	Specific Learning Disability
SLI	Speech or Language Impairment
SOL	Standards of Learning
STD	Sexually Transmitted Disease
TC	Total Communication
TBI	Traumatic Brain Injury
TD	Telecommunication Devices
TMR	Trainable Mentally Retarded
TDD	Telecommunication Devices for the Deaf
UNICEF	United Nations of International Children Emergency Fund
VRC	Vocational Rehabilitation Centre
VSMS	The Vineland Social Maturity Scale
WAIS	Wechsler Adult Intelligence Scale
WHO	World Health Organization
WISC	Wechsler Intelligence Scale for Children
Voc. ED	Vocational Education
VI	Visual Impairment

A

Abacus

Abacus is a device used by visually impaired children for doing basic mathematical calculations.

Abasia

Incoordination in walking.

Abaxial

Out of the Axis line.

Abducens Nerves

The sixth pair of cranial nerves.

Aberration

Deviation from normal.

Ability

Proficiency in carrying out various skills, understanding or adjustments. It is either general or specific.

Abnormal

Deviating from the normal.

Abortion

Expulsion of the embryo from the uterus during the first three months of pregnancy.

Acalculia

Inability to count, resulting from a cerebral lesion.

Acatalepsia

Dementia; Impairment of mental functioning.

Acatamesthesia

Inability to respond normally to auditory or visual sensations because of mental disorders.

Acataphasia

A form of aphasia which affects the manner in which words are arranged sequentially. It is attributed to brain lesion and not to psychogenic factors.

Acceleration

Acceleration is a strategy which is used when a student demonstrates competencies, knowledges, abilities and/or skills which exceed that, which is outlined in the planned course or test for his/her chronological or grade placement level. This can be determined by advanced work demonstrated in the classroom and pre- or diagnostic-tests in the skill areas. It should be emphasized that it is student who has accelerated him/self through a combination of incidental or intended learning. The districts role is to identify the level of acceleration and make the appropriate educational adjustment in placement and place.

Accessory Muscle

An auxiliary muscle which assists in the movements of the major muscle with which it was associated.

Ache

An intense, throbbing pain.

Achievement

Accomplishment or performance; the realization of potential.

Achievement Tests

A technique of psycho diagnosis revealing the extent to which subjects have mastered specific knowledge, abilities and skills. These tests reveal what the subject has already mastered, rather than generalized skills devoid of concrete content and resulting from variegated life experiences. There are three types of achievement tests, namely, action tests, written tests and oral tests.

Achloropsia

Green blindness or deuteranopia.

Achondroplasia

Defects in the cartilage at the epiphysis of long bones; hence children with this disorder have difficulty in locomotion.

Achromatic Vision

According to the duplicity (duplex), theory of vision (J. Von Kries 1894), the response which is mediated by the rods.

Achromatopsia

Total color blindness. Only rod vision exists in the achromatopsic individual hence capacity to distinguish among the grays, from white to black, with insensitivity to hues.

Acomon

The incus, or anvil; one of the three small bones of the middle ear.

Aconative

An act which lacks purpose, meaning or drive.

Acoumeter

Apparatus for determining auditory thresholds.

Acoupedic (Unisensory) Approach

This comprises use of one sense/hearing alone with suitable hearing aids.

Acousmatamnesia

Inability to learn, retain and recall or recognize sounds.

Acoustics

The science of sound; concerned with hearing.

Acoustic Immitance Assessment

Acoustic immitance screening procedures have been applied to screen infants. The use of higher probes frequencies (above 226 Hz) for obtaining the tympanograms has been suggested. This testing technique is especially well suited for children since it is objective, accurate, quick, easy to administer and creates little discomfort for the child.

Acovasm

A subjective noise in the ears (tinnitus aurium). It may be due to impacted cerumen of air pressure in the middle ear, blocked eustachian tubes, quinine, or inflammation of tympanum or middle ear. Over stimulation at given pitch (as in factory) may be a cause for some acousmas (akoasm).

Acquired Character

A trait acquired in the lifetime of the organism.

Acquired Hearing Loss

The term indicates that the hearing mechanism was normal at one time and hearing loss developed at a later stage due to some reasons like illness, accidents etc.

Acquired Immuno Deficiency Syndrome (AIDS)

AIDS is caused by Human Immuno Deficiency Virus or simply HIV. HIV infection primarily attacks the immune system, eventually rendering cell mediated immunity ineffective. This can lead to dysfunction in a number of organ systems. The common problems causing disability relate to immobility central and peripheral nervous system involvement, myopathies, bony involvement, lymphoedema, pain and psycho-social illness.

Acro

End or extremity.

Acrocephalia

A condition in which the head is normally high (vertical plane).

Acrocephaly

Distortion of the skull, giving the head a steeple shaped appearance; oxycephaly.

Acroesthesia

Hyper sensitivity in hands or feet

Acrokinesis

A feeling of extreme vigor in arms and legs; hence the hysterical individual with this symptom is hyperactive in swinging the limbs.

Acromegaly

A hyperactivity disorder in which toes, fingers and facial bones are enlarged; the nose is thickened and the lower jaw becomes enlarged. This condition was described by Pierre Marie (1880). The dysfunction occurs after age of twenty and the physical changes take place gradually.

Activities of Daily Living (ADL)

Everyday skills; the person needs to learn to function eating, dressing, bathing, hygiene skills, communication skills; Refers to the skills necessary to live independently, for example, washing clothes, paying bills, cooking etc.

Acuity

Keenness of sensation.

Acute

Sudden onset and lasts a short period of time.

Acyanopsia

Type of color blindness in which blue is confused.

Adaptive Behaviour

The individual's ability to act appropriately in social situations and to take care of their personal needs. The behaviour which is considered appropriate for a given individual in a specific context. The American Association on Mental Retardation defines adaptive behaviour as, "the effectiveness or degree with which the individual meets the standards of personal independence and serial responsibility expected of his/her and culture group".

Addison's Disease

An adrenal dysfunction in which the principal symptoms are a wasting away of tissues and great weakness restlessness anxiety, apathy, headache and vertigo are often mentioned as symptoms.

Adduction

Moving the limbs towards the midline of the body.

Adenoma

A tumor.

Adiadokokinesis

Inability to make co-ordinated successive movements, such as arm or finger movements. This condition occurs in cases of cerebellar lesions.

Adjustment

Confrontation to the environment achieved by an organism's structure, functions, organs and cells. The aim of adjustment processes is to maintain homeoslasis.

The act of or adjusting or condition of being adjusted; act of bringing into proper relations, regulation (Paley);

Adjustment is the outcome of the individual efforts to deal with stress and met his needs (Coleman);

Adjustment is a continuous process of satisfying one's needs, rather than something fixed or static and it involves virtually all aspects of human behaviour (Munn);

In a special sense of observations and measurements, the modification on weighing of a series of results to compensate for or meeting special conditions (James Drever);

The process of harmonizing behaviour with the physical and social environment. It is the process by which the person achieves satisfying relations with the people and things around him. A well-adjusted person has good relations with all the people with whom he has to interact in social situations, he modifies his habitual behaviour to accommodate the changes in the environment. Integrated personality and proper education are the two important pre-requisites for the development of adjustment abilities. The aim of education, according to some educationists is to prepare the individual for proper adjustment (P.M. Lohithakshan—Dictionary of Education—A practical approach).

Adrenal Cortex

External portion of the Adrenal gland.

Adrenal Gland

Endocrine glands located adjacent to the kidneys. The adrenal medulla secretes adrenalin (epinephrine) in states of intense emotion; the adrenal cortex supplies a hormone known as cortin. Deficiency of cortin may result in Addison's disease (1855).

Adrenal Medulla

Inside core of the adrenal gland.

Adventitious

Acquired after birth, accidental.

Adrenalin

Hormone of the adrenal medulla having a stimulating effect on the sympathetic nervous system; epinephrine.

Affective

A term which refers to emotions and attitudes.

Affective Disorder

Any disorder that affects your mood (depression, bi-polar disorder, anxiety, panic).

Affective Psychosis

A psychotic reaction in which the pre-dominant feature is a severe disorder of mood or emotional feelings. Can be related to a major depressive or bipolar disorder.

Age Appropriate

Within the child's chronological age.

Agenesis

Defective maturation as a result of hereditary or adventitious factors.

Age Norms

Numerical values representing typical or average performance of various age groups.

Aggression

A behaviour intended to hear someone or to injure that for which one stands; and the strength of aggression is inversely proportional to the intensity of frustration.

Aggression may be expressed in a generalized hostility towards society as a whole (Psychopathic behaviour) or towards a scape-coat (minority groups) as well as towards the person or persons actually responsible for the frustrations.

Agitation

Restlessness, inability to concentrate or remain motionless.

Agitophasis

Excessive rapidity of speech as in hyper kinetic hysteria or manic excitement.

Agnosia

Impairment of perception associated with certain brain lesions. Several forms of Agnosia are distinguished: optical, tactile and auditory.

Agrammatism

A type of aphasia in which the ability to speak or write grammatically has been lost or seriously impaired. The disorder was named and defined by Friedel Pick (1867-1926) as having an organic (cerebral) basis.

Agraphia

Absence of ability to express thoughts in writing. It is caused by lesions in the occipital lobe.

Air-Borne Gap

Decibel difference between the air conduction thresholds and the bone conductive thresholds in one ear (usually 10 or more than there is a conductive problem).

Alzheimer's Disease

Presenile Brain disorder that eventually results in a loss of all intellectual abilities.

Akinesis

Reduced voluntary movement, A condition of defective muscular coordination as a result of either of organic pathology or neurasthenia, self-consciousness and the like.

Akoasm

Subjective noise in the ear due to changes in air pressure in the middle ear, blocked eustachian tube, impacted cerumen, pathology of the organ of corti, changes in the liquid in the inner ear or similar causes. It is also known as tinnitus aurium.

Alalia

Inability to speak because of paralysis of the muscles used in speech.

Albinism

Children with albinism are sensitive to light due to loss of pigment in the iris and retina of the eye.

Alcoholism

A chromic disorder characterized by dependence on alcohol, repeated excessive use of alcoholic beverages, development of withdrawal symptoms on reducing or ceasing alcohol intake, morbidity that may include cirrhosis of the liver and decreased ability to function socially and vocationally.

Alerting Devices

These are devices that use sight, touch, sound or vibration to make individual's aware of an occurrence.

Alexia

Inability to read as a result of brain pathology. The condition was defined by Wernicke (1974). Various forms of Alexia are recognized as associated with the localization of the lesion.

Alienation

Falret's term (1837) to denote mental disorder.

Alogia

Inability to speak. Some writers restrict the term to denote conditions arising from organic lesions; others use it to refer to hysterical conditions as well.

Alpha Rhythm—(Berger Rhythm)

The spontaneous electrical rhythm of the brain discovered in 1924 by Hans Berger. It is the 10 per second rhythm, the amplitude of which is between 10 and 75 mv. And which appears in a developed form at about age 9 or 10.

Ambidexterity

Proficiency in the use of either the left or the right hand.

Ambilateral

Affecting both sides.

Amblyopia

The child does not use her/his eyesight in one eye (lazy eye);

Amblyopia refers to reduced visual acuity, usually in one rather than both eyes, which can not be corrected by lenses.

Ambulatory

The ability to move around without assistive devices. It may include the use of crutches, canes and other mechanical aids.

Ametropia

A general term for all conditions of imperfect retinal images due to refractive defects in the eye.

Amnesia

Loss of memory due to specific local lesions of the brain. Its two most common forms are retrograde amnesia and anterograde amnesia. Retrograde amnesia refers to inability to recall events antedating the onset of the disorder (trauma etc); it extends backwards to include events that occurred several hours, days or sometimes year prior to the cause of memory disturbance. Anterograde Amnesia refers to the inability to form memories of events subsequent to the onset of the disorder. The most severe forms of Amnesia were described by the Russian neurologist Sergei Korsakov, and are known as Korsakov's Syndrome.

Amniocentesis

It is a process which involves drawing of amniotic fluid through per abdominal route. The fluid is then subjected to biochemical and cellular tests. Amniocentesis is indicated in suspect cases of foetal chromosomal aberrations, congenital metabolic errors and open neural tube defects and severe Rh in compatibility. Amniocentesis is a technique for early identification and primary prevention.

Amentia

Mental Retardation.

Amplifier

Part of hearing aid that increases the Intensity or loudness of sound.

Amplitude of Light Wave

The vertical distance from bare to crest, which determines the intensity of the visual sensation (Titchener, 1896).

Ampulla

The enlargement at the end of a canal, as at one end of each of the semi-circular canals or at the end of the tear duct.

Amputation

Absence of all or part of limb.

Anabolism

The constructive phase of metabolism, as contrasted with katabolism.

Anacamptometer

Apparatus for measurement of the strength of reflexes.

Anacroasia

A type of aphasia in which spoken language is not comprehended but the same words, when read by the patient are understood. It is the result of a cerebral lesion.

Analgesia

Loss or total absence of the pain sensation. Analgesia may be achieved by taking an analgesic or by fixing attention on objects unrelated to the cause of pain (music etc) as well as by suggestion, self suggestion, hypnosis.

Analytical Mode or Style

One type of conceptual style based largely on a breakdown and analysis of the smallest component parts or units of any problem or idea.

Anamnesis

The history of the patient's life upto the time of the onset of mental disorder. Catamnesis is the history of the patient during the period of the mental disorder.

Anamoly

Any obvious deviation from type/normal; Irregular structure or function.

Anarthria

Loss of ability to articulate words as a result of a cerebral lesion.

Anecdotal Report

A written form of continuous data recording which provides as much information about the behaviour and the environmental surrounding as possible. The events contained in the report are then sequenced identifying each behaviour, its antecedent and its consequence (Albert and Troutman 1982).

Anemia

A deficiency of blood or a lack of a red corpuscles or hemoglobin.

Anencephaley

Absence of cerebral tissue.

Anesthesia

Absence of sensation, especially of pain. It may be general or local, psycogenic or organic.

Aniseikonia

Disparity in the size of retinal images.

Anismetropia

Inequality in the refractive mechanism of the eyes.

Ankle Clonus

Alternate rigidity ands release of tension in calf muscles when the foot is suddenly dorsiflexed. The condition is indicative of lesion in the spinal cord.

Ankylosis

Immobility in a joint because of ossification of cartilage.

Annual Goals

A required component of IEP. Goals are written for the individual student and can be for a maximum of one year.

Anomic

Individual or group norm of behaviour.

Anopia

Blindness because of pathology in the eyes (not because of lesion in the nervous system).

Anopthalmos

No eyeball.

Anorexia

Loss or lack of appetite for food.

Anoxemia

Deficiency in the oxygen content of the blood, with accompanying symptoms of disturbances in mental functions.

Anoxia

Deficient amount of oxygen in the tissues of a part of the body or in the blood stream supplying such a part.

Antagonism of Muscles

The opposition of action in two sets of muscles, the one being relaxed while the other is tensed.

Anterior (Ventral)

Front of the body.

Anterior Fonanel

The soft spot on the top of the head that usually closes over by 18 months.

Anti-Convulsants

Medications to control seizure.

Antimetropia

Refractive disparities in the eyes. Astigmatism might affect one eye, and near sightedness the other.

Anxiety

An emotional state arising in situations of impending danger and manifested in expectation of unfavourable events. Unlike fear as a response to a specific threat, anxiety represents generalized, diffuse or pointless fright. Anxiety may manifest itself as a feeling of helplessness, uncertainty of oneself. Lack of sufficient strength in the fact of external factors and exaggeration of their potency and threat.

Anxiety Disorders

Disorders in which anxiety is a characteristic feature or the avoidance of anxiety seems to motivate abnormal behaviour.

Apathy

Morbid indifference; A condition in which zest for the life is lost.

Aphasia

Loss of the ability to understand or express languages because of accident or illness; A broad term subsuming the loss of various speech functions as a result of cerebral lesions. Broca (1861) discovered the site of a cerebral lesion in the brain of a man who had lost the ability to speak more than a few words for about three decades. Several classifications are used, including of expressive and receptive, congenital and acquired aphasia.

Aphemia

Broca's term for loss of ability to speak as a result of cerebral lesion (1861).

Aplasia

Failure of an organ to develop as a result of congenital factors (Primary aplasia), or disease in infancy (Secondary aplasia).

Apraxia

Loss of specific habits as a result of brain lesions; Difficulty controlling voluntary muscular movements with usually no motor or sensory impairment.

Apthongia

A speech disorder resulting from muscular spasms of the tongue.

Aptitude

A capacity in any given skill or field of knowledge, on the basis of which a prediction may be made regarding the amount of improvement which further training might affect.

Aqueous Humor

The liquid in an anterior chamber of the eyeball (the space between the cornea and the lens).

Areflexia

Absence of reflexes or suppression of certain reflexes as a result of lesions.

ARIA Braille Operated Portable Taling Calculator

It is the size of video cassette and has features like word-processing, note taking, clock and calendar, diary, telephone directory with tone dialer. This device promotes the independence of user (visually impaired) in learning.

Army Alpha & Beta Tests

The measures used (1917-1918) to appraise the intelligence of recruits in the Army of the United States. The alpha was devised for English speaking literates; the Beta for non-English speaking soldiers and illiterates.

Arterisclerosis Cerebral

Chronic inflammation of the muscular wall (intima) of articles of the brain (hypertensive encephalopathy).

Arthritis

Inflammation of a joint; It is characterized by pain, swelling and limitation of joint movement. There are many types of arthritis such as Oster arthritis, Rheumatoid Arthritis.

Articulation

Movements of the vocal organs made during production of speech sounds; pronunciation of words and sounds.

Articulation Disorders

Difficulty with the production of speech sound.

Art Therapy

A type of psychotherapy using art as a therapeutic device.

Ascending

Running in a cephalic direction.

ASHA

American Speech Language Hearing Association, also the name of the monthly journal dealing with news, announcements and professional matters.

Aspiration

An initially motivated, sensually experienced need for or attraction towards an object. Depending on the degree of subject's awareness; Aspiration as a dynamic tendency takes the form of a drive or desire.

Assessment

Assessment means gathering information about a person and his environment to solve problems; Assessment refers to process of gathering and analyzing information in order to make instructional, administrative and/or guidance decisions about or for an individuals (Wallace, Larsen & Elksnin, 1992).

Assessment Team

A team of people such as psychologist, speech pathologist, physician, audiologist etc. who test the child.

Assistive Listening Devices

Hearing aids and other equipment that help people make better use of their residual hearing are assistive listening devices.

Assistive Technology

Technology used to help a person with disabilities.

Astigmatism

A refractive disorder due to defects in curvature of cornea, lens or eyeball. Blurred vision caused by uneven curvature of lens or cornea.

Astigmatometer

Apparatus for measuring the degree of astigmatism.

Asthma

A breathing disorder.

Asymmetrical

One side of the body is different from other.

Asynergia

A condition of incoordination among muscles which normally function in unison.

Ataxia

A poor balance, condition in which there is no paralysis, but the motor activity cannot be coordinated normally; Muscular system incoordination caused by lesions in the nervous system. It usually indicates pathology in the extra-pyramidal motor system.

Athetoid

Characterized by difficulty with voluntary movements, especially in controlling those movements in desired direction. Unwanted jerky repetitive or purposeless movement.

Athyria

Absence of thyroid or cessation of thyroid activity.

Atonicity

Reduction of the contraction of muscles; flaccidity of posture.

At Risk

Children who may or may not develop problems in their development that will affect their learning process.

Atrophy

Degeneration of organic structures; Degeneration of muscles.

Atroply

Degeneration of tissues.

Attention

Activity of a subject concentrated at a given moment on some real or ideal object (thing, event, image, discourse etc.).

Attention Deficit Hyperactivity Disorder (ADHD)

Individual exhibits poor attention, distractibility, impulsivity and hyperactivity; Attention deficit hyperactivity is also called Hyperkinesis. The cardinal features of this disorder are extreme and persistent restlessness, sustained and prolonged motor activity and difficulty in maintaining attention.

Attention Span

The length of time a person can concentrate on a singular activity before losing interest.

Atresia

The atresia means absence of external ear. More often congenital atresia is accompanied by the anomaly of the middle ear as well.

Attitude

A subject's readiness or predisposition in anticipation of a definite object (or situation); A mental set to respond to a situation with a prepared reaction.

Attitude Scale

A device used to compare individuals by extent, strength and stability of their attitude to a given phenomenon.

Audiogram

The written results in a graph form of a hearing test measured in decibel (loudness) for each frequency (pitch).

Audiologist

A specialist in hearing disorders and remediates hearing problems.

Audiometer

Audiometer is an electronic device producing pure tones. It measures the Hearing Threshold Level (HTL); Hearing Level (HL) and Sound Pressure Level (SPL).

Auditory Brainstem Response (ABR)

A hearing test usually used with babies or other hard to test patients. The patient is usually asleep or lying very still. Electrodes measure resting brain waves and when sound is made. Tumors and other specific medical problems that may affect the person's hearing, may be discovered.

Auditory Discrimination

Ability to detect differences between sounds of different frequency, intensity and pressure pattern components; Ability to distinguish one speech sound from another.

Auditory Nerve (Acoustic Nerve)

Eighth cranial nerve of vertebrates, innervating inner ear.

Auditory Organ

Sense organ for detecting sound.

Auditory Perception

Ability to attach meaning to what is heard.

Auditory Training
A method for teaching children to make full use of their hearing ability; hearing to optimize residual hearing by focusing on sounds in the persons environment.

Augmentative Communication
Special devices that provide an alternative for spoken language.

Aura
The forewarning which some patients have before onset of a grand mal convulsion.

Autism Spectrum Disorder
Any disorder that falls under the category of "autism" from high functioning (often called Asperger's Syndrome) to serve mental retardation along with specific characteristics of non-interaction in the social environment and developmental delays that are characteristic of autism.

Auricle
The outer portion of the ear (Part of external ear).

Autism
Morbid pre-occupation with oneself together with indifference to other people and with a tendency to retreat into pathological fantasies.

Automatic Nervous System
The part of the peripheral nervous system that carries messages between the central nervous system and the internal organs.

Aversion
Unpleasant attitude towards a person or a situation, with a tendency to withdraw.

Aversive Stimulus
A stimulus which a person tends to avoid if at all possible.

Avoidance Behaviour

Those response emitted by the individual with the intent of avoiding or postponing an aversive stimulus.

Awareness

Consciousness of stimulation.

Axon

The process of nervous which transmits the nervous impulse from the cell body to the next dendrite.

B

Babble Stage
Period of simple vocalizations which the normal infant uses in play at about two months of age.

Backward Child
Euphemism for a child of subnormal intelligence. Backwardness however may be caused by adventitious factors, such as, timidity, malnutrition, illnesses, uncorrected sensory defects, cultural impoverishment of the environment and the like.

Baryecoia
Partial loss of hearing.

Baryencephalia
Stupidity.

Baseline
Beginning observations prior to intervention, level of functioning established or measured without any active intervention from the observer. The current level the child is functioning at before instruction.

Basic Skills
Reading, writing and arithmetic.

Basilar Membrane

The lower side of the membranous cochlea upon which lies that organ of corti. This membrane separates the scala vestibuli from the scala tympani in the cochlea of the inner ear.

Battery of Tests

A group of measures designed to appraise various abilities of a person in order to determine fitness for employment or to assist in counselling.

Behaviour

Any observable, measurable and recordable movement, response on verbal or non-verbal act demonstrated by an individual.

Behaviour Checklist

A list of non-academic behaviours with a rating scale. Used by teachers, parents or other adults in order to diagnose students as having a disorder such as ADHD (Attention Deficit Hyperactivity Disorder) or SED (Serious Emotional Disturbance).

Behaviour Modification

A technique of changing human behaviour based on the theory of operant behaviour and conditioning. Careful observation of events preceding and following the behaviour in question is required. The environment is manipulated to reinforce the desired responses thereby bringing about the desired change in behaviour.

Beta Movement

Type of apparent movement in which two visual stimuli presented at optimal distance and time seem to combine into a single movement. It was described in 1913 as a result of further investigation of the Wertheimer phenomenon (1912).

Bharati Braille

The phonetic based Bharati Braille codes were evolved for use in India in 1951. It is uniform Braille script for all the Indian languages.

Bilateral

Affects both sides of the body.

Bilingual

Using or able to use two languages in varying degree of proficiency.

Bilingualism (in Education of Deaf)

The deaf children should first be given an opportunity to learn sign language of their deaf community, and they could be taught the language of the society.

Binaural

Pertaining to both ears.

Binet Test

Comprehensive scale of Intelligence.

Binocular Vision

Pertaining to both eyes; the use of two eyes to see a single image.

Biovulaz Twins

Fraternal Twins, dizygotic twins.

Birth Hemorrhage

Referring to a rupture of blood vessels in the brain of an infant during the process of birth. It is mentioned as a possible cause for certain personality disorders and deficiencies.

Birth Trauma

Shock of birth; Rank's Theory (1923) that birth itself is a traumatic experience and that the anxiety of psychoneurotics recapitulates the psychological concomitants of birth.

Blind (Legally)

Having central visual acuity of 20/200 or less in the better eye after correction, or visual acuity of more than 20/200 if there is a field defect which the widest diameter of the visual field subtends on angle distance no greater than 20 degrees.

Blind Spot

The area of the retina where the optic nerve enters. It was discovered by Mariotte in 1668.

Blocking

Difficulty in recollection or interruption of a train of thought or speech.

Body Image

Mental image one has of his own body; The concept and awareness of one's own body as it relates to orientation, movements and other behaviour.

Bone Conduction

A method of stimulating the hearing mechanism of the inner ear through apparatus transmitting the vibrations to the cochlea. If the lesion is in the tympanum or the middle ear, the patient is able to hear by this technique.

Borderline Intelligence

The level of intelligence above that of the moron and below that of the dull normal. Terman (1916) set the intelligence quotient between 70 and 80.

Brachycephaly

The word brachycephaly comes from the Greek brachys, short + kephale, head; A short head, one that is short in diameter from front to back. Brachycephaly is a frequent feature of syndrome of congenital malformation (birth deficit complexes) including Down Syndrome (Trisomy 21).

Brachymetropia

Near sightedness.

Bradylalia

Abnormal slowness in speech.

Bradylexia

Abnormal slowness in reading.

Bradyphrasia

Extreme slowness in talk as a result of a brain lesion.

Braille

Braille is a basic system of reading and writing for the blind. It consists of six dot cell that provides for sixty three different characters. 26 combinations of dots are used for 26 letters of the alphabet. The remaining 37 combinations represent punctuation signs and contractions that allow for shortening or abbreviating words. In some ways, Braille is a system of shorthand since each word is not spelled out letter for letter. A pattern of raised dots that are felt with fingers to help the blind read.

Braille Master

This is a machine which does automatic Braille translation from Braille to normal letters and vice versa. It allows both visually impaired and sighted person to operate as it contains the key boards of both the normal typewriter and mechanical brailler.

Brain

The brain contains more than 90 per cent of the body's neurons. Physically, the brain has three distinct areas that are evident from earliest development within the embryo. From the back to the front of the head, they are the hindbrain, midbrain and forebrain. Hindbrain is made up of the cerebellum, pons and medulla. The midbrain lies between the hindbrain and forebrain. The forebrain consists of the thalamus, hypothalamus and cerebral cortex.

Brain Injured Child

A child who before, during or after birth has received an injury to or suffered an infection impairment, there are disturbances which prevent or impede the normal learning process.

Brainstorming

Problem solving strategy in which an individual or a group collects numerous ideas and evaluates them only after all ideas have been collected.

Brightness

Intensity of a visual sensation. It is dependent upon the degree of saturation and upon the intensity of illumination.

Bulb

Medulla oblongata.

C

Caccias

Total blindness.

Cacergasia

Mental deficiency.

Cachexia

Condition of malnutrition and general weakness as a result of drug addiction.

Cacopathia

The most serious mental disorders. The term is attributed to Hippocrates.

Cacophonia

Harsh, unpleasant voice, as in laryngitis or other pathologies of the vocal mechanism.

Campimeter

(Perimeter): Apparatus for mapping colour zone of the retina. Aubert (1857) first reported on the differential sensitivity of various parts of the retina and Landolt (1872) described more completely the differential sensing of various hues on the parts of the retina.

Cardiac

Pertaining to the heart.

Cardiograph

Apparatus for recording heart beat.

Case History

Reconstruction of the past life of an individual (normal or abnormal) in order to determine the underlying causes for present behaviour.

Catabolism

Disintegration of tissues. It is the antithesis of anabolism, which is the repair of tissues or constructive metabolism.

Cataract

Loss of vision due to a cloudy vision; In cataract, the lens which is transparent in nature becomes opaque and the light rays are absorbed.

Categorization

The ability to sort objects by function, colour, size, group etc.

Catharsis

The release of tension and anxiety of recounting and/or acting out past experiences.

CAUD Test

Thorndike's battery of tests (1926) which measure academic intelligence, the following specific abilities being appraised: completion, arithmetic, vocabulary and directions.

Cell

The unit of organism (Sah Wann 1839).

Central Hearing Loss

This is an abnormality in the Central Nervous System from brain damage or disease.

Central Nervous System (CNS)

The brain and the spinal cord. The part of the nervous system to which the sensory impulses are transmitted and from which motor impulses develop.

Cephalgia

Headache.

Cephalic Index

Ratio of Breadth and length of the skull.

Cerebellar Ataxia

Lack of integrative synergia in voluntary (striated) muscular activity. The condition arise from a lesion in the cerebellum. Locomotor is uncertain and wobbly (cerebellar gait), and the muscles do not function in reciprocal innervation.

Cerebellum

Brain structure related to the control of movement & body coordination.

Cerebral Dysohythmia

Abnormal rhythm of the brain waves.

Cerebral Palsy

Motor disability associated with organic brain damage or malformation; A disorder of the central nervous system which affects muscle movement. Cerebral palsy is not a disease, nor it is hereditary.

Cerebrum

The two lobed structure growing as an extension of the brainstem.

Cervical

Pertaining to the region of the neck.

Chain Reflex

An automatic type of response in which the response constitutes the stimulus for a second response, and so on.

Chorea, Huntington's

A severe disorder which makes its onset at about age thirty or forty and is characterized by an increasing rate of choretic movements, with great mental deterioration.

Chromatic Aberration

The result of unequal refraction of light from various parts of the spectrum.

Chromosome

A minute body in the cell. In mitosis, the chromatin is resolved into the chromosomes which contain the genes (determiners of heredity).

Chronic

Pertaining to a condition which progresses slowly and is long continued.

Chronological Age

The age of a person in years. It is compared with mental age to determine the IQ score of a person. $IQ = \frac{MA \times 100}{CA}$.

Cilia

Hair like processes whereby certain protozoa move about; also, hair-like processes on certain epithelial tissues.

Ciliary Body

The part of the vascular tunic of the eyeball between the choroids membrane and the iris, whereby the accommodation of the lens is mediated. Muscle fibres in the ciliary body contract and pull the body forward.

Cleft Palate

An opening in the roof of the mouth; Congenital fissure of the soft palate and roof of the mouth, sometimes extending through the premaxicilla and upper lip.

Close Circuit Television (CCTV)

CC TV is very useful for the education of low vision children. The system includes an inexpensive television camera which is focused on the reading material. The enlarged images of the letters then appear on an ordinary television set or monitor. The control of the movement of the camera and the magnification, intensity and contrast of the image is under the control of the reader.

Closed Captioning

The deaf/hearing impaired are able to watch TV program, movie or video by reading words printed on the screen.

Closed Caption Decoder

A device that makes captions appear on a television.

Cochlea

The cavity of the inner ear which makes 2½ turns and is about one inch long. The organ of corti (containing the receptors) lies in the cochlea. It is shaped like the shell of a snail and is approximately a quarter inch from front to back.

Cochlear Implant

Cochlear implant is the relatively new form of assistive device for the profoundly deaf who receive little benefit from conventional acoustic aids. The development of cochlear implant has enabled the direct electrical stimulation of remaining auditory nerve fibres, thus by passing non-functional or absent hair cells in the cochlea.

Cognition

All the intellectual activities, as distinguished from conation and affectivity.

Cognitive Modelling

This approach is directed towards providing learning disabled children with an awareness of how people learn or remember. In cognitive modelling, the learning disabled child is exposed to models (adults or peers) who tend to be more reflective so that he can imitate the model and learn the appropriate strategy.

Cognitive Style

A certain approach to problems-solving, based on intellectual, as distinguished from affective, schemes of thought.

Collapsible Cane

This cane is made of a special grade of aluminum tubing which can be directly formed into conical numbers. This technique called swaging requires a very special machine, a swaging machine. This enables the persons with visual impairment to adjust according to their height. It is also easy to carry this device.

Colour Blindness

Inability to discriminate colours. Achromatopsia (total colour Blindness) is rare; Dyschromatopsia (partial colour blindness) occurs in 4 to 7% of males and 0.5% females. Deuteranopia is green-blindness; protanopia, red-blindness. The phenomena of colour-blindness (Daltonism) were first described by John Dalton (1974).

Coma

State of unconsciousness from which the individual cannot be aroused by orders or other external methods.

Commissural Fibres

Nerve fibres which unite the two hemispheres of the brain or the two sides of the spinal cord.

Communication

Communication is the activity or process of giving information to other people or to other living things, using signals such as speech, body movements or radio signals.

Community Based

A standard by which special education services may be judged, skills are taught at varied locations in the community rather than in the classroom in order to facilitate generalization and application.

Compensation

According to Adler, the person's effort to effect or overcome imagined or real personal weaknesses.

Complex Tones/Sounds

Complex tones are sounds that contain more than one pure tone in a systematic manner. The wave form will be periodic. There will be a pattern in the way the various pure tone are combined and hence the resultant sound is pleasant to hear.

Comprehension

The ability to understand something fully.

Compression

Reducing the amount of visual information sent in a signal by only transmitting changes in action.

Compulsion

Unwelcome repetitive action; A repetitive act that an individual cannot consciously control.

Conation

A term introduced by Ward (1886) to denote that part of the mind which is implied by such words as willing, desire, aversion, motivation and the like.

Concentration

The act of focusing attention upon a restricted range of elements in a total situation these elements contributing to the achievement of a purpose or need of the individual.

Concept

A logical form of thinking; the highest level of generalization, characteristic of verbal-logical thinking concept may be concrete or abstract. The most abstract concepts are called categories. An abstract idea generalized from particular instances. It involves idea of the existence of objects, processes or relation of objects, i.e., table, cell, man, raining famine etc,

Conductive Hearing Impairment

A dysfunction of the outer or middle ear in the presence of a normal inner ear is termed as a Conductive hearing impairment. The conductive hearing loss can be congenital or acquired. A temporary or permanent hearing loss which occurs when something interferes with the passage of sound to the inner ear.

Cones

Receptors in the retina which respond in daylight vision (Von Kries 1894). These cells were first identified by Kolliker (1854) as differing from rods.

Confabulation

A person replaces memory loss by a fantasy.

Conflict

In psychoanalytic sense, a condition of psychic tension resulting from a repressed wish or from ambivalent instinctual drives. Allport (1923) differentiates between conflicts between two or more persons (overt conflict) and the struggle between rival impulses within the individual (Covert conflict)

Congenital

Existing from birth; a condition that is present at birth.

Congenital Hearing Loss

The condition of hearing loss existing since birth. Congenital loss may be hereditary or may develop during prenatal or natal period.

Congenital Myasthenia

Deficiency or loss of muscle power.

Conjunctivitis

A painful eye disease which causes the thin skin that covers the eyeball to become inflamed.

Conjunctival Hyperemia

Condition in which the eyes have a blood shot appearance.

Connectors

The nervous mechanisms which mediate between receptors and effectors.

Conoid Body

The pineal body.

Consanguinity

Blood Relationship, descent from a common ancestor.

Consciousness

The supreme level of mental reflection of objective reality, inherent in man exclusively by virtue of his socio-historical essence. Consciousness is a continually changing totality of sensory images and thoughts that arise directly before the subject in his inner experience and anticipate his practical activity.

Constancy of the IQ

The tendency of the intelligence quotient to remain unchanged between successive tests of the same individual over a period of years.

Convergent Thinking

Thinking that is directed toward one correct solution to a problem; Thinking which results in conventional solutions and answers or conformity. Contrast with Divergent thinking.

Convulsion

Pathological muscular contraction.

Coping Mechanism

Techniques that tend to help us deal with anxiety. Usually a conscious process that provides sufficient relief, e.g. exercise, humour.

Cord

A tendon; the spinal cord.

Cornea

The transparent area (one-sixth the surface circumference) in the anterior of the eyeball. It is continuous with the sclerotic membrane.

Corneal Ulcer

When the foreign body stays in the cornea, it may lead to ulcer which in turn reduces the vision from mere blurring to total blindness. Corneal ulcers are developed in the eye due to bacteria, virus infection, fungus, hypersensitivity reactions, vitamin deficiency etc.

Correlation

Correlation is concerned with describing the degree of relation between two variables (Ferguson). There are three types of correlations—positive, negative and zero.

Cortex

Outer or surface layer of the brain or other organ.

Corticosterone

Hormone of the adrenal cortex.

Counselling

Advice given by a professional.

Covert

Concealed or disguised.

Cranial Anomaly

Abnormal structure of the bones of the head.

Cranio Stenosis

Premature closing of the cranial structures.

Creativity

It is the ability to invent and develop new and original ideas, especially in artistic way.

Creative Thinking

The achievement of a new relationship among the parts of experience which according to the Wallace (1928) has four stages; Preparation, Incubation, Inspiration or Illumination and verification. The creative idea (third stage) comes as a flash of insight or a sudden thought.

Cretinism (Thyroidinism)

Mental and physical retardation resulting from thyroid insufficiency during fatal life or early infancy.

Criterion—Referenced Test

A test used to determine a child's level of achievement. Once this level is established, a criterion or goal is fixed for the child to achieve. Child is evaluated according to own performance, not in comparison to others.

Critical Ratio

The difference between two normally distributed sets of scores divided by the standard error.

Critical Score

The score on a test (or battery of tests) which separates the unsuccessful from the successful candidates for preferment (as for a job).

Cry Epileptic

The sound made by the sudden expulsion of air from the lungs of the grand mal patient in the initial phase of an attack.

Cryptogenic

Of unknown origin.

Cued Speech

Method of communication used by some persons with hearing impairments. It is used to reduce the ambiguities involved in lip reading. This method is caught in the controversy between teaching deaf children to rely on oral methods of communication or to use sign language. The system was invented by Dr. Orin Cornett in 1966. In English, the system uses 8 different hand shapes in 4 different locations near the mouth. The shape and locations in combination with the mouth movements represent the exact spoken sound thus helping to eliminate the ambiguity of speech reading. The hand shapes represent the consonants, the location shows the vowels. Placement of hand shape in a location is indicative of the complete syllable. It has to be used in conjunction with spoken language and thus takes the guess work out of speech reading.

Culture Free Test

A type of test that has been constructed to minimize bias due to ethnic background or to the differing experiences of children raised in rural rather than urban culture or in lower class rather than middle or upper class cultures.

Curriculum Based Assessment

A methodology of increasing importance in special education in which a child's progress in the curriculum is measured at regular intervals.

Curve; Normal Probability

The graphic representation of the theoretically possible distribution of an infinite number of scores which vary by chance having a bell shaped appearance.

Cytomegalic Inclusion Body Disease

Infectious condition in which a maternal virus infects the fetus; may be associated with mental retardation.

D

Dactylomegaly

Abnormally large fingers.

Dark Adaptation

The adjustment of the eye to a low intensity of light (Aubert, 1865).

Day Blindness

Low visual acuity in daylight as a result of scotoma, nutritional disorder, or other conditions affecting the sensitivity of the retina.

Deaf

Hearing impairment which is so severe that the child is impaired in processing linguistic information through hearing, with or without amplification which adversely affects educational performance.

Deaf Blind

Concomitant hearing and visual impairments, which cause such severe communication and other developmental and educational problems that they cannot be accommodated in special education programmes solely for deaf or blind children.

Deaf-mute

A person unable to hear or to speak, other than by unintelligible gutturals.

Debility

General weakness (asthenia).

Decerebration

Removal of the cerebrum.

Decibel

One tenth of a bel; hence a convenient unit for measuring intensity levels of sounds loudness level.

Defense Mechanism

Ways an individual protects himself from emotions that are too uncomfortable.

Deficit

A level of performance lower than expected for a child; Inadequacy in functioning due to general immaturity, developmental lag and irregularities.

Dehydrated

Lacking in water.

Delay

Development which does not occur within expected time ranges.

Delayed Response

A response which ensues after a time interval has elapsed following the application of the stimulus.

Delirium

Mental disturbance resulting from fever intoxication, disease or trauma; A mental state characterized by disorientation and confusion.

Delusion

Belief contrary of reality and held in spite of evidence and common sense.

Dementia

Impairment of mental functioning. Primary dementia involves intellectual under development caused by a hereditary disease, harmful innate factors, or by early childhood deprivation. Secondary dementia results from an atrophy of mental functions caused by lack of exercise, emotional support and the constant influence of harmful factors (social, age, medical disease related).

Dendrite

The short branch of the nerve cell which conducts the impulse to the axon.

Depression

Melancholia, gloom, dejection; An emotional state of despondency characterized by negative emotional attitudes, a change in the motivation sphere, cognitive; impressions and generally passive behaviour.

Depth Perception

Visual perception of a person at different distances; Depth perception refers to the ability to perceive three dimensional world through the aid of perceptual cues. It is also referred as the ability to perceive the solidity of objects and their relative position in space.

Desire

Feeling of want transformed into an active thought about possessing or accomplishing something.

Deterioration

Continuous impairment of a function or the totality of functions. It is marked by loss of interest, poor social adjustments, or faulty ethical behaviour as well as by reduction of physical vigour.

Developmental Disability

A condition that prevents a child from developing normally which results in mental retardation or Autism; A condition a person is born with that causes him not to develop normally. They usually have a lower IQ than those not born with this.

Developmental Tests

Tests that compare a child's development to others of the same age.

Developmentally Delayed

A child who acquires skills after the expected days.

Developmental Norms

Age at which an average individual achieves some developmental milestone.

Developmental Reading

Pattern and sequences of normal reading growth and development in a child in the learning to read process.

Deviate

One whose behaviour or physique differs markedly from the average.

Deviation

The distance of a score from some measure or reference point, such as mean mode & median.

Dextrality

Handedness, or preference for the use of the right side more than for the other in motor activities.

Diagnosis

Identification of a disease or disorder; It refers to the effort to establish the cause of a condition and to outline appropriate treatment implied by that condition.

Diagnostic Test

One which assists in the location of specific difficulties or pattern of errors. In educational psychology, a diagnostic test is used to appraise the specific disabilities of a pupil in a given subject and thus to furnish a basis for remedial instructions. Diagnostic achievement tests are most commonly prepared for the skill subjects—reading, arithmetic, spelling.

Diabetes Mellitus

Physical disorder characterized by an excess of sugar in the blood and other organs; associated with a disturbed insulin production.

Dichromatopsia

Red and green blindness.

Diplegia

Paralysis affecting both sides of the body; Paralysis of legs and arms with the legs more seriously affected.

Diplopia

A condition of muscular imbalance in which one object is seen as two.

Disability

A physical or mental problem that prevents someone from functioning at a normal rate; Disability refers to the effect of impairment on the individual such as the movement difficulties associated with cerebral palsy.

Disorder

A Generic term for any pathological condition.

Disorientation

Loss of awareness of the position of the self in relation to space, time or other persons; Confusion about time place & person.

Disposition

According to Mcdougall (1923), the totality of the instinctive tendencies of an individual; The subject's readiness to a behavioural action or to a sequence of actions.

Distractability

Over-responsiveness to extraneous stimuli; Inability to concentrate or attend to the task on hand; Inattentiveness.

Distress

A state of extreme unhappiness or worry.

Divergent Thinking

Fluency, Flexibility, originality and elaboration are the elements of divergent thinking; Thinking which results in novel, unique or creative solutions or answers. Contrast with convergent thinking.

Dizygotic Twins

Those which are result of fertilization (By spermatozoa) of two separate ova. Monozygotic twins (identical) are the result of fission of a single fertilized ovum; Fraternal twins, biovular twins.

Dolichocephaly

Long narrow head; having a cephalic index of 77.6 or less. The cephalic index is the ratio of the breadth of the skull to the length. Some writers refers to skulls above 80 as brachycephalic; those below 80 as dolichocephalic.

Dominant Character

That which suppressed the recessive character (Mendel, 1866).

Down's Syndrome

A child with chromosomal abnormalities which often results in mental retardation; This is the second largest genetic (but not inherital) cause of intellectual disability. (Howard et al. 2001; Mazzocco 2 O' Connor 1993). It is caused mainly by the existence of a third 21st chromosome (termed trisomy 21) or, in 5-10% of cases, by translocation of extra chromosomal material to another chromosome (Howard et al. 2001). Less obvious is the mosaic Down Syndrome, in which 10-12% of the individual's cells have the extra genetic material.

Dpoamine

Chemical involved in the transmission of nerve impulse.

Due Process

A procedure to help/protect the rights of children with disabilities; In general due process includes the elements of notice, opportunities, to be heard and to define one's self; Procedures used if parents disagree with any findings, recommendations regarding identification, evaluation or educational placement for their child, or if special services are inadequate.

Dyscalculia

A learning disability in which a child is unable to do math problems.

Dysfluency

A break in the smooth flow.

Dysfunction

Abnormal or imperfect functioning of an organ.

Dysgraphia

A learning disability which impairs the child's ability to write.

Dyskinesia

Impairment of power to make voluntary movements; Disturbance of voluntary muscular reaction.

Dyslalia

Disorder of articulation.

Dyslexia

Inability to read; A disorder of children who despite conventional experience, fail to learn to read. The term is most frequently used when neurological dysfunction is suspected as a cause of the reading of disability; Learning disability affecting reading ability. Persons with dyslexia may have difficulty remembering, recognizing, and or reversing written letters and words might read backwards, and have poor hand writing.

Dyslogia

Inability to express thoughts in understandable speech.

Dysmnesia

Impairment of memory functions.

Dysmorphia

Misshaped body; Dwarfism, gigantism, acromegaly and the like.

Dysopia

Generic term for many grave pathology of the eye or the accessory apparatus of the eye.

Dysphasia

Impairment of ability to speak clearly as a result of cerebral lesion; Disharmony between different regions of the body.

Dysphonia

An unnatural sound to the voice.

Dyspraxia

Impairment of well-established habits as a consequence of a stroke or of other pathologies of the central nervous system.

Dystrophy

Impaired growth.

E

Early Intervention

A process used to recognize warning signs for disability and to take early action against factors that put individuals at risk. Early intervention can help children get better in less time and can prevent problems from becoming worse.

Ear Mould

The ear mould is a plastic or silicon insert designed to conduct the amplified sound from the hearing aid receiver into the ear canal.

Ear mould is a device which couples the hearing aid to the ear canal. This is a very important component of the hearing aid as this will ensure that all the amplified signal is directed into external ear canal. It is very important that the ear mould fits well into the ear.

Echolalia

Repetition of the exact words spoken by someone else.

Echopathy

A disorder characterized by senseless repetition of words or of actions by others. The patient seems to have a morbid compulsion to imitate.

ECHO II Speech Synthesizer

This plug-in unit converts most correctly spelled words to speech output. The user may select pitch level and rate, and has words said aloud or spelled letter by letter. Punctuations and numbers can also be pronounced by this system.

ECT

Electro Convulsive Therapy.

Ectomia

Excision, as of a portion of the brain.

Electro Encephalogram (EEG)

A recording of the brain's waves, it measures the output of the brain.

Edema, Cerebral

Excess fluid in the ventricles or outside the brain substance and within the membranes covering the brain.

Educable Mentally Retarded

Education term used to describe retarded who can profit from academic education; mildly retarded; IQ generally from 55 to 70.

Education

An activity for passing on certain socio-historical experience to new generations; a systematic and purposeful influence that ensures the moulding of an individual, his preparedness for social life and productive labour.

Effector

A response mechanism, such as muscle or gland.

Efferent Fiber

One which transmits the nervous impulse from the brain or the cord to an effector.

Egomania

The ultimate in conceit.

Electroencephalography

Recording the electrical waves of the brain.

Electromyography

Measurement of muscle action potential.

Electro Oculography

Recording of eye movements and pupillary reactions.

Electro Shock Therapy

Treatment of a behaviour disorder by electric shock to the brain.

Embolalia

Neologisms intrspersed among the words of sentences uttered by the patient.

Embryo

Organism in the earliest phase of its development.

Emmetropia

Normal vision.

Emotion

Etymologically, the word emotion is derived from the Latin word 'emovere' which means 'to stir up', 'to agitate'. Woodworth defines—"Emotion" is a 'moved' or stirred-up state of organism. It is stirred-up state of feeling that is the way it appears to the individual himself. It is a disturbed muscular and glandular activity—that is why it appears to an external observer.

Emotional Catharsis

Emotional release through the relieving of a traumatic experience.

Emotional Lability

In psychiatry, emotional instability, a tendency to show alternating states of gaiety and somberness.

Emotionally Disturbed

Children with behavioural disorders variably designated as neurotic, psychotic or character disordered and where inabilities may manifest themselves in school accomplishment, school relationships or feelings of self adequacy and may result from experience or biological limitations.

Empathy

A projection of one's own personality into the personality of another in order to understand him better; Appreciation of another's problems and feelings without experiencing the same emotional reaction.

Encephalitis

Inflammation of the brain tissue; Encephalitis lethargical was fully described by Economo (1929) though the first reported case occurred in 1915.

Encephalon

The brain.

Encephalomalacia

Softening of the brain with concomitant impairment of mental functions.

End Brain

The Telencephalon (outerior portion of the prosencephalon).

End Organ

A term used by Von Frey (1894) to denote the mosaic of reception in the skin. (Pressure, cold, warmth & pain).

End Plate

Expansion of the motor fibres or axons on a group of muscle fibres.

Endocrine Glands

Ductless glands.

Endogenous

Developing within or originating from causes within the organism; Arising from within the body.

Endopphasia

Silent reproduction of a word or sentence without overt activity in the speech organs.

Endowment

The capacity of an individual as determined by his heredity.

Enuresis

Involuntary discharge of urine. Also known as bedwetting.

Environment Factors

Variables such as poverty, racial discrimination, school pressures and deteriorating family units.

Enzyme

Organic substance capable of producing other substances by catalytic action.

Epilepsy

Group of nervous diseases marked primarily by convulsions; A brain disorder characterized by seizures or compulsions; Convulsive disorder; A condition of cerebral dysrhythmia; A disturbance in the electrochemical activity of the discharging cells of the brain produced by a variety of neurological disorders. The causes are not clear. These electrochemical disturbances usually result in a seizure of some degrees.

(A) Petitmal—A mild form in which dizziness or staring into space takes place.
(B) Grand mal—A seizure in which there are severe convulsions and loss of consciousness or coma.
(C) Jacksonian—Spasm mainly limited to one side of the body and often to one group of nervous.

(D) Psychomotor—Patient performs motor acts which he cannot remember having done.

Epileptic Furor

Condition of excitement following a grand mal convulsion or substitute for it.

Epinephrin

Hormone secreted by the medulla of the adrenal gland.

Erb's Palsy

This condition results in paralysis of the muscles of the shoulder, arm and hand. The arm hangs limp, the hand rotates inward and normal movements are usually lost. The most common cause is nerve damage during breech birth.

Erethism

Heightened responsiveness of the nervous system; excitability.

Ergography

Kicsow's apparatus (1890) for studying the effects of muscular fatigue. In the usual form, the apparatus consists of a spring which is pulled repeatedly by the middle finger, the number and the strength of the pulls being recorded.

Etiology

Study of causes or origins of a disease; The investigation of the causes or significant antecedents of a given phenomenon; Causative factors, Predisposing and precipitating, which result in a disorder.

Eu

Greek prefix denoting a normal, healthy or desirable condition.

Euphoria

An exaggerated unrealistic sense of well being.

Eupraxia

Good muscular coordination in learned functions.

Evoked Auditory Response Audiometry (ABR)

This can be used both as a screening tool to identify the presence of hearing loss and as a diagnostic tool to quantify the degree of hearing loss. For screening an infant under 5 months of age, the ABR has emerged as the clear method of choice (ASHA, 1989).

Evoked Otoacoustic Emissions (EOAE)

EOAE is an objective, non-invasive and quick method of testing for cochlear functions. The test can be administered by less skilled persons and a high sensitivity. The most promising application to date is the use of EOAE to screen for normal or near normal cochlear status in neonates and infants.

Eyed Ness

The dominance (muscular) of one eye over the other in such activities as threading a needle, sighting a rifle, looking through the manoptoscope and the like.

Eye Movements

The saccadic movements of the eyes, as in reading a line of print.

Exceptional Child

An exceptional child is one who deviates intellectually, physically, socially or emotionally so markedly from what is considered to be normal growth and development that he can not receive maximum benefit from a regular school program and requires a special class or supplementary instruction and services.

Exogenous

Outside the genes, all factors other than heredity or genetic (such as environment or trauma).

Expressive Language Disabilities

The inability to communicate verbally.

External Auditory Canal

This is an 'S' shaped tube open at the pinna and closed in side by the eardrum. It measures about 25 to 40 mm in length and has an volume of about 4 cc.

External Control

Control for weakening behaviour to its preconditioning level.

External Otitis

External otitis is an inflammation of the skin of the external auditory canal, most frequently due to bacterial or fungal infection.

F

Facial Asymmetry

Imbalance between expressions and morphology of the right and left halves of the face, which is infrequently mentioned as a possible sign of cerebral hemisphere dominance.

Facial Expressions

Static and dynamic patterns of the face, which are important as social stimuli (F. Allport 1924).

Facial Nerve

The VII cranial nerve.

Facilitator

A leader, planner and manager of instructional activity, yet lets the students still be responsible for their own learning.

Familial

Pertaining to the family; hereditary.

Familial Trait

A characteristic which appears in successive generations of a family and which may be due to genes or to cultural influences.

Family Therapy

A specialized type of group therapy in which the members of a given family constitute the group.

Far-sightedness

Hyperopia; The condition is due to shortness of the eyeball or a defect in the lens and it is at least partially correctable by convex lenses.

Fascinating Gait

The incoordinated walk of a victim of paralysis agitans. The walk is hurried and uncertain as to direction.

Feeble-mindedness

Oligophrenia, mental deficiency.

Feedback

Return to a control centre of information regarding events under its control in psychology, the return of sensory information from the periphery used in the control of movement and analogous process, the loop of information going back from output to input.

Fenestra Ovalis

Oval shaped aperture into which the footplate of the stirrup (stapes) is inserted; Opening in the middle ear.

Fenestra Rotunda

A round aperture closed by a small membrane; a part of the middle ear.

Fetal Alchohol Synchrome (FAS)

Child may be born low weight, severe retardation and physical problems due to mother drinking alcohol while pregnant.

Fetus

Human embryo after the sixth to eighth week of pregnancy.

Field of Vision

The area of a person can see around them without moving their eyes or head.

Figure Ground Perception

The ability to attend to one aspect of the visual field while perceiving it in relation to the rest of the field.

Fine Motor

Fine motor skills can be defined as small muscle movements: those that occur in finger, in co-ordination with the eyes. For example, writing, typing etc.

Finger Spelling

Finger spelling is nothing but writing in the air with configurations of fingers. The finger spelling can be described as a manual representation of written language (Same as manual of alphabet); Hand shapes of the alphabet, a way for the deaf/hearing impaired to spell.

First Cranial Nerve

The olfactory nerve.

Fissure

Furrow or groove on the surface of the brain.

Fixation Point

Any point upon which one or both eyes are focused when motionless. Binocular fixation refers to the act of focusing both eyes simultaneously, and it was first described by J. Muller (1826). Fixation time refers to the interval for which the eye is stationary while the individual is engaged in the act of reading.

Flaccid

Limp; without normal tonus; Completely relaxed muscles.

Flexor Muscle

A muscle that bends flexes a limb.

Fluorosis

Fluorosis, caused by excessive amount of fluoride in drinking water may eventually lead to crippling. Though untreatable, it can however be prevented by checking drinking of high fluoride water and eliminating consumption of food items, drugs and toothpaste which contain excess fluoride.

Focus of Eyes

The act of binocular adjustment on a central point so as to effect clear, fused retinal images. The near point of accommodation for normal eyes is a fixation point on the median line about three inches distant from the face.

Folic

French term for an adventitious mental disorder.

Folic Du Doute

Chronic indecision, abulia.

Fontanelles

Un-ossified areas on the cranium of the neonate.

Forebrain

Uppermost portion of the brain.

Form-board

A measure of intelligence which consists of blocks to be fitted into a recess. The first form board was devised by Seguin (1842), and many types have been constructed by subsequent investigators.

Formal Assessment

Formal Assessment involves the use of standardized tests, which demands a high degree of uniformity in administration and interpretation. Formal tests are generally of three kinds—(1) General intelligence and aptitude test (2) General achievement tests (3) Personality tests.

Fovea Centralis

The depression in the macula lutea which (in the human eye) contains no rods, and which is the point of clearest vision.

Fracture

The most common condition due to trauma is the fracture. This group is usually subdivided into simple (no external wound), compound (broken bone with an external wound leading to the site of the break), or comminuted (splintered bone).

Fragile X Syndrome

It occurs when a long arm of the X-chromosome becomes detached or connected to the rest of the chromosome by only a thin strand. This condition is now considered to be the leading hereditary cause of intellectual disability, being transmitted from generation to generation in a complex fashion (Batshaw 1997; Howard et al. 2001).

Frequency

Cycles/second, It is measured in hertz-hz the number of times a sound wave vibrates in a second. The human ear can hear frequencies from 20 Hz to 20,000 Hz. The frequencies which are less than the human audible frequency are called as subsonic frequencies and those which are above the human audible range are called as Ultrasonic frequencies.

Frustration

Psychological state resulting from the blocking of goal directed activity. It manifests itself in sensations of oppressive stress, worry, despair, anger etc.

Frustration Tolerance

Level of one's ability to accept frustration.

Functional Disorder

A term loosely used to refer to disorders which do not have a demonstrable organic etiology.

Fusion

Fusion refers to the ability to perceive two dissimilar images seen by each eye as one single mental image. In other words, the power of co-ordinating the images received by the two eyes into a single mental image is also called as Fusion.

G

Gait

Manner of walking. The following types of gaits are often mentioned (in clinical psychology); Ataxia (the foot being raised high and brought down on the whole sole), Cerebellar (staggering), Cow (caused by known-knees), Frog (hopping manner of the victim of poliomyelitis), Paretic (shuffling), Spastic (feet scarcely raised, toes dragging, legs almost unbent), Waddling (duck-like manner of victims of certain type of paralysis).

Galactosaemia

Condition marked by an accumulation of galactose in the blood stream; may be associated with mental retardation.

Gamete

A germ cell.

Ganglion

Group of nerve cells, bound together by connective tissues, which lie outside the brain and spinal cord.

Ganglion Cells

Group of nerve cells usually located outside the brain and spinal chord.

Ganglion

Nerve Centre.

Gargoylism

Gross abnormalities in bony structure of the body, opaque corneas, enlargement of the liver and speech together with mental deficiency (described by Fredgold, 1912).

Gene

The bearer of heredity, which lies in the chromosome.

Generalization

In concept formation, problem-solving, and transfer of training, the detection by the learner of a characteristic or principle common to a class or objects, events or problems. Also in conditioning, the principle that once a conditioned response has been established for a given stimulus, other similar stimuli will also evoke that response.

Generalized Reinforcers

Use of tokens, points and money to reinforce behaviour.

Genetic Code

Chemical pattern in the DNA molecule which determines the physical structure of the DNA.

Genetics

The biological study of Heredity.

Genius

A broad term referring either to an abnormally high order of general intelligence.

Genotype

The sum total of all the genes localized in the chromosomes of a given organism. In a broader sense, Genotype is the sum total of the organism's genes inherited by parents. This term was introduced in 1903 by the Danish biologist Wiehelm Johannsen.

Geriatrics

Branch of medicine which deals with the physical disorders associated with advanced age.

Germ-cell

Weismann's term (1893) for the reproductive cell which preserves a continuity in spite of changes occurring in the somatic cells.

Gifted

Having superior mental ability or intelligence.

Glau Coma

Increased intraocular pressure; hardening of the eyeballs. The degree of interference by glaucoma in vision, varies from slight blurring to complete blindness.

Glia Cells

Supporting cell in the nervous system.

Glioma

Intrinsic tumor of the brain tissue.

Glutamic Acid

Enzyme having anticonvulsive properties.

Grade

A grade is a symbol (a number or a letter) that summarizes the level of students work.

Grade Skipping

Promotion to a higher grade often confused with acceleration. A grade skipped.

Grand Mal

Major convulsive seizure.

Grand Mal Seizure

Severe epileptic seizure which often results in a loss of consciousness.

Grandiose Delusions

A delusion in which the individual believes he or she possesses great importance, power, wealth or intellect.

Gray Matter

The cortex of the cerebrum and the inner portion of the spinal cord.

Gross Motor

Co-ordinated movements of all body parts; for example, trunk, shoulder and neck.

Group Dynamics

Group Dynamics is the field of study within the social sciences that focuses on the nature of groups. The group dynamics may also include changes in behaviour of a person when he is represented before a group, the behavioural pattern of a person vis-à-vis group.

William Schutz (1958, 1966) looked at inter-personal relations from the perspective of three dimension: inclusion, control and affection. This became the basis for a theory of group behaviour that see groups as resolving issues in each of this stages in order to be able to develop to the next stage. Conversely, a group may also devolve to an earlier stage if unable to resolve outstanding issues in a particular stage.

Group Norms

Standards of behaviour accepted in a given community and governing human relationship. Group norm allow a person to assess his own and other people's actions, compare them with models, choose the necessary norms of behaviour and drop out those unacceptable to a given community and guide and control his relations with other people.

H

Habilitation

Improvement in a skill or level of adjustment as with respect in the ability to maintain satisfactory employment.

Hair Cells

Processes in the Organ of corti (and elsewhere in other organs) which are responsive to stimulation; hair like process of sensory nerve endings.

Hallucination

Perception without an appropriate stimuli.

Handedness

Preference for the use of one hand more than the other in various activities. A dextrosinistral individual is one who, having a preference for using the left hand, has been taught to write, draw, hold a fork, throw and the like, with the right hand. The index of dextrality refers to a ratio of preference for right or left hand in a variety of tasks.

Handicap

A physical or mental problem that prevents some from functioning at a normal rate; Impairment of a particular kind of social and psychological behaviour. It is the extent of the individual's subjective interpretation of his disability and impairment; Handicap is the social stigma and environmental restrictions that are often imposed on those with disabilities but which are not usually on inevitable feature of their conditions.

Handy Braille

Handy Braille is a software used for producing Braille materials in all Indian languages. This software does not require a translating package. The regular keyboard can be used to input the data and the data entry is made through six dot Braille mode. Braille dot configuration appears on the screen of the computer and therefore, correction can be made easily.

Haplopia

Normal fusion of retinal images, focus accommodation. This condition is the opposite of diplopia.

Hard of Hearing

Hearing impairment, whether permanent or fluctuating, which adversely affects a child's educational performance.

Hearing Aid

Any device which amplifies or focuses sound waves in the listener's ear, usually refers to the various types of wearable amplifiers which operate with miniature loudspeakers in the ear or oscillators on the head.

Hearing Loss Degree

(a) Mild—27-40 dB—Person will have difficulty with faint or distant speech, may need favourable seating and may benefit from speech reading, vocabulary, and/or language instructions or may need speech therapy.

(b) Moderate 41-55 dB—Person can understand conversational speech at a distance of 3 to 5 feet, probably will need a hearing aid, auditory training, speech reading, favourable seating, speech conversation and speech therapy.

(c) Moderately severe—56-70 dB. Conversation must be loud to be understood, speech will probably be defective, may have limited vocabulary, may have trouble in classroom discussions; services used in moderate level; only specific assistance from the resource/itinerant teachers language area needed.

(d) Severe—71-90 dB—Person may hear loud voice at one foot, may have difficulty with vowel sounds but not necessarily consonants; will need all services mentioned and use many techniques used with the deaf.

(e) Profound 91 dB—May hear some sounds; hearing not primary learning channel, needs all mentioned services with emphasis on speech, auditory training, language; may be in regular class part time or attend classes that do not require language skills.

Hemeralopia

Blindness or indistinctness of vision in sunlight. The condition is associated with albinism, malnutrition, deterioration of pigment cells in the retina, general weakness, and similar pathologies.

Hemi

Greek prefix referring to an unilateral condition.

Hemiablepsia

Unilateral or bilateral blindness is one-half of the visual field, as a result of lesions in the optic commission.

Hemianacusia

Unilateral deafness.

Hemianopia

Vision in only one half of the visual field.

Hemiataxia

Inability to effect muscular co-ordination on one side of the body; as a result of lesion in the nervous system.

Hemiplegia

Paralysis of one side of the body.

Hemophilia

A condition, usually hereditary, in which the blood does not coagulates when the individual is cut.

Heredity

A broad term referring usually to the sum total of biological influences which at the time of conception determines an individual's capacity for growth and development.

Heroin

Narcotic derived from morphone.

Herpes

Red spots in the skin due to inflammation of small blood vessels. The condition is said to occur in some individuals as result of intense emotional stress.

Hertz (Hz)

The pitch of the sound, the number of vibrations per second; A unit of vibration frequency adopted internationally to replace the term cycles per second, named Heinrich Rudolf Hertz: German physicist.

Hetero

Greek prefix which signifies others, different.

Hetrometropia

A condition of refractive disparity between the two eyes.

Heterogenous Grouping

An educational practice in which students of diverse abilities are placed within the same instructional groups. This practice is usually helpful in the integration of children with disabilities.

Hexadactylism
Having six fingers or toes.

Hind Brain
Lower brain structure including the pons, medulla and cerebellum.

Histamine
Chemical mediator in the transmission of the nerve impulse.

Homebound Instruction
A teacher provided to students unable to attend school.

Homogeneous Grouping
An educational practice in which students of similar abilities are placed within the same instructional groups. The practice usually serve as a barrier to the integration of children with disabilities.

Hormone
Chemical substance secreted by the endocrine glands; Secretion of an endocrine gland.

Hospital and Homebound
Students within chronic conditions that require long term treatment in a hospital or students who are home bound and receive special instructions from homebound d/itinerant special education personnel.

Hydrocephalus
Increased volume and pressure of cerebrospinal fluid in the ventricles of the brain; A type of mental deficiency resulting from an excess production of cerebrospinal fluid in the ventricles of the brain. The head is usually very large, general physical condition is poor, and the mental defect varies from idiocy to borderline. The exact cause is unknown.

Hyper
Greek prefix which denotes "an excess of" or "an unusual amount of".

Hyper Acusia

Abnormal keenness of hearing.

Hyperactivity

Hyperkinesis, Excessive motor activity or restlessness; A personality disorder of childhood or adolescence characterized by over-activity, restlessness, distractibility and limited attention span.

Hyperacuity

An exceptionally low threshold of stimulation in any or all sense organs.

Hyperalgesia

Extreme sensitivity to pain.

Hyperanakinesis

Rapid twitchings in a limb or the facial muscles.

Hyperaphia

Textile sensitivity in an extreme degree.

Hyper Asthenia

Extreme weakness.

Hyperemia

Increased amount of blood in the part of the body.

Hyperesthesia

A low threshold for stimulation of sense organs.

Hyper Kinesis

Excessive muscular action.

Hypermnesia

Remarkable ability to retain, recall and recognize past experiences; Occurs irrespective of a person's intellectual ability and is met even in feeble minded. May also appear in response to the stimulation of drugs, fever brain injuries and electric stimulation of certain areas of cerebral cortex. Hypermnesia may also occur in hypnotic state and in ordinary dreams.

Hyperopia

Farsightedness; difficulty seeing near objects; Hyperopia is that state of refractive power of the eye which occurs when the principal focus lies behind the retina.

Hyperphasia

A rapid, incoherent jumble of words.

Hyperpyrexia

The word hyperpyrexia denotes an increase in body temperature of more than 105 degree F. Associated disorientation, fits, unconsciousness may be present. If left untreated, there may be prolonged coma or fits which cause permanent residual disability.

Hyperpituitarism

Acromegaly, which is a condition marked by a large head, thick lips, prominent nose, large chest, short arms and legs and huge hands.

Hypertension

High Blood pressure.

Hypertonicity

Increased muscle tone.

Hyperthyroidism

Over-activity of the thyroid glands; Excess activity of the thyroid gland which causes loss of weight, hyperhidroses, irritability and hyper tonicity.

Hypoglycemia

Lowered blood sugar; The normal brain usually utilizes only glucose for its metabolic requirements. Hence hypoglycemia is manifested principally as CNS (Central Nervous System) dysfunction.

Hypo Kinesis

Lethargy; under-activity.

Hypoplasia

Under development of part of the body.

Hypotonicity

Decreased muscle tone consistently; Extreme difficulty moving or holding pastures against gravity; weak survival reactions (e.g. Gag reflex).

Hypothyroidism

Thyroid under-activity. Any condition leading to the deficient production of the thyroid hormone is called Hypothyroidism.

Hysterical Deafness

Psychogenic hearing loss; a functional hearing impairment developed under emotional stress as an unconscious means of escape from intolerable situations. Same as conversion deafness.

I

Ideophrenia

A mental disorder with strong obsessional trends.

Idiot

The lowest grade of mental defective. Binet defined idiocy as a condition of such want of intelligence that the individual can make no use of language and that his aptitude are roughly equal to these of a two-year old normal child or less.

Imagery Types

Galton's conclusions (1883) regarding the incidence of various types of mental images (visual auditory, gustatory, motor, olfactory, tactual) which were reported to him in response to his famous questionnaire.

Images

An image is a mental representation or recollection of a sensory experience. Image allow us to use concrete forms to represent complex and abstract ideas.

Imbecile

According to the well known definition of the Royal Commission on the Feeble minded; "One who by reason of mental defect existing from birth or from an early age, is incapable of earning his own living but is capable of guarding himself against common physical dangers." Binet (1908) states that imbeciles cannot write intelligibly or read with comprehension and that the level of intelligence does not exceed that of a normal child of six or seven years of age.

Immature

The condition of not yet having attained full growth. Immature behaviour usually refers to that which is inappropriate for the individual's level of chronological development.

Immediate Memory

The repetition of a list of words or digits without error after a single presentation. Jacob (1887) was among the first to determine experimentally the immediate memory span.

Implicit Behaviour

Subdued muscular activity as contrasted with overt behaviour. According to Watson (1919), thinking is a process of implicit behaviour, such as lip and tongue movements, slight gesture and the like.

Impulse

A sudden drive to action; particularly a relatively simple drive of short duration. It is a sudden and intense drive.

Impulsivity

To respond carefully considering alternatives.

Incidence

Incidence is defined as "the number of new cases occurring in a defined population during a specified period of time".

Inclusion

Inclusion assumes that most children are best served in regular settings (including schools, homes and community services) as this is where they will need to exercise their daily living skills

(Guralnick et al. 1995). It refers to a pluralistic system where there is not a focus on accommodating children with a typical needs within programs but on designing programs that can support all children, whatever their needs (New and Malloy 1994, Salisbury 1991).

In Inclusive education approach, the special education is an integral part of the general education system. In Inclusive education, three types of services are provided directly or indirectly to the disabled child. The most essential services are provided by the general classroom, teachers and parents as well. Use of the assistances of non-disabled children is vital in the inclusive education; Varied degrees of inclusion are practical in schools. Full inclusion is the practice of educating all children in regular classrooms and schools regardless of disabilities.

Incoordination

Inability to control muscular movements in purposeful activities such as walking, writing, speaking or standing.

Incus

This is small anvil shaped little bone with the same length and weight as the malleus. The head of incus is attached to the head of the malleus.

Individual Differences

The measurable unlikeness of people, which, in a random sampling of any given trait, provides data for a bell-shaped curve.

Individualized Education Plan (IEP)

A programme drawn up by a professional team of experts. It includes assessment, instructional goals and kind of educational services to be provided.

Infancy

The first eighteen months of life.

Infantile Autism

Childhood Psychosis.

Inferiority Complex

In Adler's theory, the condition by which an individual is emotionally paralyzed by fueling of inferiority.

Informal Assessment

Informal methods of testing are non-standardized procedures used by teachers and other professionals to collect information about the learner.

Informal Reading Inventory

A procedure for assessing a child's level of reading competence consists of a series of graded passages.

Inheritance

The transmission from one generation to another:

(a) social institutions, culture, mores and folkways, personal advantages arising from the privileged states of parents and the like and
(b) of the genetic constitution which determines physical growth and development.

Inhibition

Restraint or control exercised over an impulse, drive or response tendency.

In-home Interventions

Special education services delivered in a child's own home. This is sometimes done to facilitate generalization for children with cognitive disabilities and to generalize self control strategies for children with behavioural problems.

Impairment

Impairment in medical perspective means the damage to the tissues. According to World Health Organization, an impairment is a discrete loss of mental or physical functioning, such as brain damage, a missing limb, paralysis after polio etc.

Innate

Those factors present at birth which result from the genetic component inherited from the parents plus any mutations.

Inner Ear

The vestibular apparatus, semicircular canals and cochlea.

Inner Speech

Implicit muscular activity in the articulatory apparatus.

Instructional Feedback

Verbal or written information to an individual about him/her behaviour. Can be objective, descriptive or evaluative ("Goods", "Poor", "almost").

Intelligence

Intelligence is judgment or common sense; initiative, the ability to adopt oneself (Binet);

Intelligence is a general capacity of an individual consciously to adjust his thinking to new requirements (Stern);

Intelligence is the ability to carry-out abstract thinking (Terman).

Intelligence Quotient (IQ)

A measure of intellectual functioning obtained by dividing MA by CA and multiplying by 100; Stern's technique (1912) if dividing mental age by Chronological Age in order to have a convenient expression for the ratio of intelligence to actual age.

Intelligence Test

An item or series of items designed to measure the higher intellectual capacities of a person. Simon (1905) published the first practicable measure of intelligence, and Goddard (1910) adapted it for use in America.

Integration

Integration is the process of bringing 'part' (the handicapped) to the 'whole' (the society. Integration is opposite to segregation.

Intensity

In physical terms, intensity is referred to as amplitude. Amplitude is the extent of displacement of the vibratory particles in either direction from the position of rest. Intensity of sound is measured on a decibel (dB) scale. Human ear can hear sounds which are as soft as 0 dB SPL. Sound causes discomfort when it is 120 dB SPL and becomes painful at 140 dB SPL.

Intentional Act

Voluntary behaviour, as opposed to reflex response.

Interdisciplinary Team

Various individuals from different disciplines that assess individual children's need (Speech Therapist, Occupational Therapist nurse, Psychologist etc.)

Interest

The word 'interest' in Latin language means 'it matters'. Any preference displayed where choices are offered; An interest is a disposition in its dynamic aspect (Drever).

Interpersonal Relationships

The reciprocal influences which persons exert upon one another in primary (face to face) social groups.

Interpreter

A person who helps with the communication between the deaf/ hard of community and the hearing community.

Intro Version

Preoccupation with one's self, with accompanying reduction of interest in the outside world.

Involuntary Movements

Impulsive or reflex motor acts performed without control of consciousness. Involuntary movements may be of an adaptive nature (e.g. blinking), withdrawing one's hand from a painful irritant) and of a non-adaptive nature (e.g. chaotic movements in case of dulled consciousness).

Irradiation

Exposure to a large amount of radio activity, e.g. X-rays.

Iris

The pigmented circular membrane lying between the cornea and the lens of the eye.

Itinerant Teacher

This teacher travels from school to school helping the child with special needs and acting as a consultant for the regular teacher.

J

Jacksonian Seizure

Convulsive disorder in which the muscular contraction is limited to the arm, leg or face.

Jaeger Test

Measure of visual acuity in which types of different sizes are read from a card held in normal reading positions.

Jena Method

Karl Brauck Mann's technique for teaching deaf children to speak the procedure being for the children to feel lip movements and thus get kinesthetic concepts.

Jolly Reaction

Abnormal fatigability of a muscle stimulated by constant faradic current, taken as one sign of possible myasthenia gravis or after-effects of encephalitis.

Juvenile

Youth or adolescent.

Juvenile Delinquency

Juvenile Delinquency may be defined as a social offense committed by an individual, below the age of eighteen, for a number of times which if committed by an adult, would be considered and punished as a crime.

Juvenile Diabetes

Excessive sugar in the child's Hovel and urine which could cause visual impairments, coma, limb amputation, and death if untreated.

K

Kellen Helen

American Women who became blind and deaf at 18 months of age and was afterwards taught by Anne Sullivan.

Kinesthesis

The sensation of body movements; The sense of movement derived from receptors in skeletal muscles, joints etc. in the Rorschach — a movement response.

Kinesthetc Approach

A training programme that uses sensations derived from muscles or motor movements.

Knowledge

The first level of Bloom's taxonomy. Knowledge involves recalling information such as names, dates, events, places and major ideas.

Kurzweil Reading Machine (KRM)

The KRM reads printed materials, books, magazines, letters and reports. The electronic voice allows the blind students or worker to access to material that would otherwise be unavailable. The KRM can also be attached to video terminals to provide speech output; small computer convert print into synthesized speech. The material is placed face down on a scanner and is read by the "electronic voice".

L

Labial

Pertaining to the lips.

Labiograph

Apparatus for recording lip movements in speech or in thinking (Implicit speech behaviour).

Labyrinthine Apparatus

The cavities of the inner ear which include the vestibular apparatus, the semicircular canals and the cochlea.

Lacrimal

Pertaining to the ear glands.

Lalia

Speech.

Laliphobia

Dread of the necessity of speaking by a person with a speech impediment.

Lalling

Meaningless repetition of sounds as by an infant or a mental defective.

Lalopathy

Any disorder of the speech functions.

Laloplegia

Speech disturbance resulting from a stroke. The muscles of the tongue are unaffected.

Language

A system of symbols for communicating meaning; Language is a mental phenomenon, a body of knowledge about the speech sounds (vowels, consonants), meaning and syntax, which resides in the mind (brain) of the users. The term 'a language' is used to refer to all systems of speaking, writing or signing common to a group of people.

Language Disorders

Inability to understand and express ideas. Effect the person's development in other areas such as motor, cognitive or social.

Language Pathology

Study of the causes and treatment of disorders of symbolic behaviour.

Lanugo Hair

The soft, cotton like hair of the Mongoloid; also, the hair appearing on the fetus at about the fifth month.

Large Print Computer (LPC)

LPC is designed especially for low vision people. The enlarged display letters are an automatic feature with no special programme required. The LPC can be used with a variety of peripherals such as printer.

Laryngograph

Apparatus for recording movements of the larynx;

Laser Cane

Laser Cane emits three beams of infrared light which get converted into sound after they strike the object on the path.

Lateral

Away from the midline of the body.

Lateropulsion

Involuntary tendency to sway or walk to one side as in the case of an individual with organic brain disorder.

Learning

A broad term referring to modifications of behaviour as a result of experience (Gates & Others).

Learning Disability

A child with average or above average potential has difficulty learning in one or more areas (such as reading or writing or matter). And exhibit severe discrepancy between their ability and achievement; Disorder of one or more of the basis psychological processes involved in understanding or using language, spoken or written which may manifest itself in imperfect ability to listen, think, speak, read, write, spell or to do math. Inability is not due to mental retardation, emotional disturbance, or environmental disadvantage. There is a notable difference between his apparent capacity for achievement and his actual achievement.

Learning Styles

A term used to describe personality, psychological traits, social behaviours, developmental differences, communication styles, and environmental preferences (Ramsay 1991).

Least Restrictive Environment (LRE)

An educational setting which gives students with disabilities a place to learn to the best of their ability and also have contact with children without disabilities; Handicapped children are only removed from regular education environments when the severity of the handicap interferes with satisfactory participation.

Legally Blind

A visual field which is not greater than 20 degrees or visual acuity of 20/200 or less in the better eye after correction.

Lens

Convex transparent body lying posterior to the pupil and iris.

Leprosy

Also known as Hansen's disease. It is a chronic infectious disorder caused by Myco-bacterium eprae. It primarily affects skin, peripheral nerves and other organs, e.g., eyes. The common deformities seen are wrist drop, foot drop, claw hand etc. depending on the peripheral nerve involved.

Lesion

Any hurt, wound or local degeneration.

Level of Aspiration

A self imposed standard against which a person judges his own performance. Level of appreciation is an index of confidence and varies with the pattern of success or failure;.

The highest achievement one desires in a particular field. It may be in any field: academic, occupational, social, political, etc. The individual's effort towards achievement is always based on his level of aspiration. Faulty self-concept is often responsible for the fixing of unrealistic levels of aspiration which very often leads to failure and disappointment. One has to fix one's level of aspiration to commensurate with abilities, opportunities, etc. in order to succeed.

Light Adaptation

A term introduced by Lohman (1906) to designate the adjustment of the eye to continued stimulation by bright light.

Light Perception

Ability to detect presence or absence of light.

Lip Reading

The art of comprehending the speech of another through the visual interpretation of gestures, facial movements and especially lip movements. Same as speech reading.

Little's Disease

Congenital spastic cerebral paralysis; named for William John Little (1810-1894); an English Physician.

Locomotor Ataxia

A condition resulting from lesions in the posterior columns of the spinal cord, with such concomitants as intense pains, girdle-sensation, sensory abnormalities loss of knee-jerk and general in co-ordination of muscular activity.

Locus of Control

A quality characterizing a person's predisposition to attribute the responsibility for the results of his activity to outside forces (External Locus of control) or to his own capabilities and efforts (Internal Locus of control). The notion of Locus of control was proposed by the US Psychologist Julian Rotter.

Logokophasia

A form of aphasia in which spoken language can not be understood.

Longitudinal

Lengthwise, running in the direction of the long axis of the body, organ or part.

Loudness

The psychological attribute of intensity of sound; Higher the intensity louder will be the sound.

Low Vision

Impaired vision but individual is able to read print with or without magnification devices; a person with low vision is one who has impairment of visual functioning even after treatment and/or standard refractive correction and has a visual acuity of less than 6/18 to light perception or a visual field of less than 10 degrees from the point of fixations, by who uses, or is potentially able to use vision for the planning or execution of a task (WHO 1992).

M

Macrocephaly

Large headedness, with associated mental deficiencies. In macrocephaly, the skull does not bulge in lateral aspects or forehead. The brain may weigh as much as 2800 grams.

Macrocheilia

Abnormally large lips, which are usually everted.

Macrodactylism

Abnormally large fingers and or toes.

Macula Acustical

Endings of the portion of the auditory nerve extending to the utricle and the saccule.

Macular Fibers

Nerve fibers forming the central core of the optical nerve.

Macula Lutea

The yellow spot on the retina, which is the point of clearest visual acuity.

Mainstreaming

Some or all the child's day is spent in regular classroom; Least restrictive alternative, maximum integration in the regular classroom, coupled with concrete assistance for the regular teacher. The concept of mainstreaming was introduced in the Education For All The Handicapped Act (USA) 1975.

Maladjustment

Any mild disturbance of the personality in which there is difficulty in securing a satisfactory adjustment to the environment, particularly to other persons.

Malformation

Any type of abnormal growth or development in any part of the body.

Malleus

This is a hammer shaped bone in the middle ear measuring 8 mm in length and 25 mg in weight. It has a long handle, which gets attached to the Tympanic membrane at a point called as UMBO and a short handle, which is free.

Malnutrition

Deficiency in calories, proteins and vitamins.

Manipulative Skills

These include working with the hands. To work, operated or treat with or as with the hand or hands.

Mannerisms

Individualistic and differentiating patterns of behaviour whereby one person's style is distinguished from another's. Many blind children of pre-school age develop habits or mannerisms that are called blindness. Such behaviours include body rocking, head rolling, waving hands before their eyes, poping fingers in their eyes.

Manual Alphabet

It is using hand shapes to represent sounds of speech. It is like writing in the air with hand shapes for letters (Same as Finger spelling).

Mastery Learning

A model of learning in which all but a very few students are exempted to achieve over time the mastery of predetermined subject matter and skills (Taylor).

Maturation

The process of maturing or developing mentally, physically or emotionally.

Maturational Lag

A slowness in certain specialized aspects of neurological development.

Minimal Brain Dysfunction (MBD)

A controversial term used to describe a child who shows the behavioural but not neurological signs of brain injury.

Mean

Arithmetical Average, the sum of all score divided by the number of scores.

Mean Deviation or Average Deviation

The mean deviation is the mean of deviations of all the separate scores in a series taken from their mean (Cearett).

Meatus

Canal or passageway.

Mechanical Ability

Proficiency in manipulating form-boards, various devices, work samples and the like. Tests of mechanical ability often includes measures of speed of work accuracy or precision, hand-eye co-ordination, manual dexterity, and structural visualization.

Medial

Nearer to the midline of the body.

Median

A measure of central tendency where half the scores are above and half below; when ungrouped scores or other measures are arranged in order of size, the median is the midpoint in the series (Garret).

Meditation

Intensive, deep-going reflection, preoccupation with an object, idea etc. which is achieved by concentrating on one object and elimination of all factors that distract attention, both external (sound, light) and internal (physical, emotional and other tensions)

Medulla

(1) The central part of an organ, as distinguished from the cortex.
(2) Any tissues which fill certain cavities.
(3) Marrow.
(4) Bulb like structure at the top of the spinal chord forming the lowest part of the brain.

Medulla Oblongata

That part of the brain stem which lies between the pons and spinal cord.

Megalencephaly

Large headedness.

Megalopsia

Visual abnormality in which objects appear to be magnified.

Maladaptive Behaviour

Those behaviours judged as inappropriate or ineffective in a given context such as the classroom in general, such behaviours interfere with a child learning or social interaction and lead to discomfort.

Memory

Memory is described as the activity of bringing past experience to bear upon a present situation; The ability to store and retrieve upon demand previously experienced sensations and perceptions even when the stimulus that originally evoked them is no longer present.

Memory Logical

The repetition of meaningful substance of material that has been learned.

Memory, Long-Term

A sub-system of memory ensuring durable (for hours, years and sometimes decades) retention of knowledge, and also of capabilities and skills, and characterized by a great volume of stored information..

Memory Rate

Reproduction of learned material in which the factor of meaning is disregarded.

Memory, Short-Term

A sub-system of memory that ensures immediate retention and transformation of data arriving from the sense organs and from long-term memory.

Memory Span

The amount that can be reproduced accurately after one impression.

Meninagioma

Tumor arising from the membranes covering the brains.

Meninges

Membrane of the brain and the spinal chord; The outermost covering is the dura; the middle the pia; and the innermost, the arachnoid.

Meningitis

Inflammation of the membranes of brain or cord, sometimes with accompanying symptoms of mental impairment.

Meningoencephalitis

Inflammation of the brain and its membrane.

Mental Activity

Any function pertaining to the mind, such as awareness, perception, imagination, reasoning and the like.

Mental Age

Level of intellectual development in terms of the average of a particular age group; An expression of the level of performance obtained and standardized test, such as the Stanford Binet, compared with the performance of the average person of a given chronological age.

Mental Deficiency

Inadequacy of intelligence or learning capacity.

Mental Health Problem

How a person thinks, feels and acts when faced with life's situations. Mental health is how people look at themselves, their lives and the other people in their lives; evaluate their challenges and problems; and explore their choices. This includes handling stress relating to other people and making decisions.

Mental Illness

This term is usually used to refer to severe mental health problems in adults. A disease of the brain that causes unusual thoughts and emotions, including depression, feeling like you can do anything and/or not knowing the difference between reality and unreality.

Mental Image

Galton's term (1883) for "mental pictures" that may be scrutinized with nearly as much ease and prolonged attention as if they were real objects.

Mental Retardation

The child's intellectual level is measured below the average range usually below 70 on IQ tests; Significantly sub-average intellectual functioning existing concurrently with deficits in adaptive behaviour and manifested during the developmental period, which adversely affects a child's educational performance.

Mental Set

Readiness to respond in a given manner to a stimulus.

Mesocephalon

The large mass of nerve fibres which lie at the base of the brain in front of medulla oblongata. The structure includes gray matter as well as fibers which are connected with the medulla, the cerebellum, and the cerebrum.

Mesoretina

The layer of the retina which contains the rods and cones.

Meta Cognitive Knowledge

It is information about how to use learning strategies and when and why to use them.

Metobolism

Building up and breaking down of body cells.

Microcephaly

Small headedness; Abnormally small head, with associated mental deficiency. The head has a cone-like appearance, and the forehead and the chin have a marked recession. The brain is reported to weigh as little as 170 grams.

Midbrain

Part of the brain which developed from the middle of the primitive brain.

Mildly Mentally Retarded

IQ range of 50-75 formerly referred to as moron.

Minimal Brain Damage

Early term for designating children with neurogenic learning and adjustment problem. The term unsatisfactory because brain dysfunction is not necessarily due to damage.

Mirror Writing

Strephographia, a form of writing in which the characters are reversed and which can be read by holding the page before a mirror.

Mixed Hearing Loss

Individual having both sensory-neural and conductive deafness.

Mobility

Mobility refers to the capacity for being moved with relative ease. For the human being, this implies an interaction with his surroundings, to influence as well as be influenced by his environment.

Mobility Aids

(a) Sighted guide—A sighted person who takes the blind person to a destination.
(b) Dog guide—Dog used by a blind person to take him to a destination.
(c) Cane—A white or silver cane often with a red tip used for getting to and from a destination.
(d) Electronic Aids—These are usually more successful when used as a companion with the cane. Two of the more acceptable ones are the Laser cane and the Kayne Spectacles.

Modality

An avenue of acquiring sensation, the visual, auditory, tactile, kinesthetic, olfactory and gustatory modalities is the most common sense modalities.

Mode

The most frequent score; The mode is strictly defined as the point on the scale of measurement with maximum frequency in a distribution (Guilford).

Modeling

A procedure for learning in which the individual observes a model perform some task and then imitates the performance of the model. This form of learning accounts for much verbal and motor learning in young children.

Moderately Mentally Retarded

The general IQ range of 35-39, generally considered trainable.

Monaural

Pertaining to a single ear. The opposite of binaural.

Mongolism

Form of mental retardation in which the patient has the facial characteristics of a member of a Mongolian race; associated with the disturbance of the Chromosomes.

Monocular

Pertaining to vision using a single eye; a disorder affecting but one eye.

Monophasia

A type of speech pathology in which utterance is reduced to a single word or sound.

Monoplegia

Paralysis involving a single limb of the body.

Monotonia

A pathology of the voice which results from paralysis of laryngeal muscles and in which inflections are consequently absent.

Monozygotic Twins

Uniovular twins; identical twins.

Mood

A feeling state or prolonged emotion that influences the whole of one's psychic life.

Morale

Zest for living, enthusiastic, devotion to group endeavour.

Moron

The mental defective who intelligence is above that of an imbecile but below that of borderline defective.

Morphology

The study of rules regarding word formation usually roots, prefixes and suffixes.

Morpheme

It is the minimum meaningful unit of language that is, the smallest unit of meaning.

Mosaicism

Chromosome disorders related to some cases of mental retardation.

Motherese

Also known as 'parentese' or 'infant elicited behaviour'. It is a form of language which adults reserve for talking with young children. In this pattern, adults speech is usually enunciated clearly and slowly, with varied pitch and intonation, with clear pauses between utterances, with emphasis placed on important words.

Motivation

An individual's level of desire to perform a specific task; A stimulus to action; something (a need or desire) that causes one to act.

Motor Development

The ability to move effectively within the environment.

Motor Nerve

A nerve fiber which transmits the nerve impulse to a muscle or gland.

Movement

Movement is a motor action in which muscles act so as to bring about required motion. This results in changes in the alignment of the entire body or any part/parts of the body. The entire body or its part/parts actually move.

Multi-disciplinary Evaluation

The information compiled by the multi-disciplinary team which describes a student's academic functioning, academic and social behaviour, learning problem and strength and educational needs; using several disciplines and instruments to evaluate a student.

Multi-disciplinary Evaluation Team

A team of specialists such as a speech and language pathologist, psychologist, occupational therapist, used to help determine the students needs.

Multi-handicapped Children

Children having more than one impairment; Concomitant impairment which causes severe educational problems that cannot be accommodated in special education programme solely for one of the impairments (excludes deaf blind).

Multimedia

Multiple forms of communication such as text, audio and/or video.

Multiple Intelligence

Theory formulated by Howard Garderner to describe the broad range of capabilities used by solving problems and creating tings and ideas.

Multiple Sclerosis

Degeneration of the central nervous system due to a progressive deterioration of the protective sheath surrounding the nerves.

Multi Sensory

Generally applied to training procedures which simultaneously utilize more than one sense modality.

Muscle Tone

The amount of tension in the muscles at rest.

Muscular Dystrophy

Destroys muscle tissue which leads to a progressive deterioration of the body; This term represents many genetic conditions that cause progressive loss of muscle tissue and subsequent muscle weakness, which first shows in the early childhood years following normal motor development during infancy. Progressive physical disability occurs during childhood and with the commonest form (Duchenne dystrophy), death usually occurs in the late teens as a result of heart or respiratory failure, although other forms of the disease have longer lift expectancy (Howard et al. 2001). Being X-linked, the condition affects mainly boys.

Mutism

Inability, or want of desire, to speak.

Myadriasis

Pathological enlargement of the pupil.

Myasthenia Gravis

Muscular weakness without atrophy. This child usually functions better upon rising and weakens with repetitive use of muscles during the day.

Myelin

The white substance which covers the medullated nerve fibres. This sheath was described by Schwann, a German Anatomist; hence it is often called the substance of Schwann.

Myesthesia

Sensitivity to muscular contractions.

Myograph

Apparatus for recording involuntary muscular movements or tremors.

Myopia

Near sightedness; Blurred vision with distant objects harder to see than near objects. In this condition, parallel rays of light are brought to a focus in front of the retina, i.e. before reacting the retinal surface.

Myxedema

Condition thought to be due to thyroid pathologies which is accompanied by muscular weakness, tremors, dullness, slowness of reaction time and general lethargy.

N

Nanism

A form of dwarfism in which the head is proportionately large and the rest of the body stunted. It is thought to be due to endocrine dysfunctions.

Native Language

The child's primary language.

Nausea

Visual distress with tendency to regurgitate.

Negative Feedback

Communication to the subject that his response was incorrect. It tends to reduce the chances of repetition of the behaviour.

Negative Reinforcement

A procedure for strengthening behaviour when the consequence of that behaviour is the termination or avoidance of an aversive stimulus. That is, the response is followed by the avoidance or termination of some event noxious to the individual

Nemeth User's Mathematical Braille Effortless Reproduction System by Raised Dot Computing (Numbers)

In this system, both text and mathematical equations entered from a Braille device can be printed out in English on a special dot matrix printer with the use of this software. When learning mathematics at the higher education level is considered difficult, the NUMBERS raise the hope about the possibilities of learning abstract concepts of mathematics by children with visual impairment.

Neoadrenalin

Chemical mediator in the transmission of the nerve impulse; Norepinephrine.

Neologism

A child makes up words that only have meaning to them.

Neonatal

Period between onset of Labour and several months after birth.

Neonate

The infant from birth upto one month of age.

Neoplasm

Any new growth of tissues which serve no physiological function, such as cysts, tumors and the like.

Nerve Impulse

The change (electro chemical) which moves from the dendrite to the axon and thence to the dendrite of the next cell or to the tissues of the effector.

Nervous System

The totality of nerve formations in animals and humans with which they perceive the irritants that act on the body, work off the excitations occurring therewith and develop reactions. The nervous system ensures the functioning of the organism as a single whole. It includes the central, peripheral and vegetative nervous systems.

Neuroglia

The cells which form the supportive tissues of the nerve cells in the cerebrospinal system.

Neurolinguistics

It studies the brain mechanisms of speech and the changes in speech processes that arise at a result of local brain lesion. The forming of neurolinguistics as a discipline is linked with the development of neuropsychology, on the one hand, and linguistics and psycholinguistics, on the other.

Neuron

The nerve cell with all its extensions, the main structural unit of the nervous system.

Neuoriticism

A state characterized by emotional instability, anxiety, low self respect, and vegetative disorders. Neuroticism should not be identified with neurosis, since neurotic symptoms may be shown by healthy individuals too. Neuroticism is generally assessed by special scales or personality inventories.

Night Blindness

The individual with night blindness experiences blurred vision and progressive constriction of the visual field.

Non-organic Hearing Loss

The hearing loss that is not due to physical impairment in auditory systems is called non-organic loss. The cause of this loss is rather psychological than anatomical. This loss is also referred as psychogenic or functional hearing loss.

Non-verbal Communication

Non-linguistic aspects that contribute to the effect of the spoken message include facial expression, eye contact, gestures, body posture, head and body movement, manual sign, writing, drawing or representational symbols (Banburye Hebert 1992).

Norms

A standard of reference in making judgments; an average common or standard performance under specified conditions; Statistics that describe the test performance of specified groups, such as pupils of various ages and grades in the standardization group for a test. Norms are often assumed to be representative of some larger population, as of pupils in the country as a whole. Norms are descriptive of average, typical or mediocre performance, they are not to be regarded as standards or as desirable levels of attainment. Grade, age and percentile are the most common type of norms.

Norm Referenced Test

A standardized test in which the performance of the individual is interpreted in relation to the performance of a group of others who are the same age and ability.

Noise

Unpleasant, non-periodic sound waves.

Nystagmus

Spasmodic oscillations of the eyeballs. The disorder occurs in albinos and colour-blind persons frequently and it is also found in individuals with certain types of organic pathologies.

O

Object Pemanence

The child is aware that an object still exists even when it is taken away.

Objective Observation

Audiotape, videotape or written notation of behaviours. Can include tallies for frequency, duration or speed. Can be a narrative transcription of the actions and verbalizations observed.

Observation

A principal empirical method in psychological research, which involves systematic and purposeful perception of behavioural or mental phenomena aimed at studying their specific changes in certain conditions and to finding their meaning.

Obsessions

A thought or action that a person does over and over again; A persistent repetitive and unwanted thought. Cannot be eliminated by logic or reasoning.

Occipital Lobe

The posterior part of the cerebrum (in either hemisphere).

Occupational Therapy

A program of creative educational and recreational activities to develop skill which will be useful later; Originally the use of diverting, interesting activities to help the patient pass the time in a hospital or institution; now, the use of activities which may be necessary adjuvants to the medical care (such as those which exercise certain muscles, afford release for tensions, prepare the patient for re-employment, for release and so on.

Occupational Therapist

A therapist that focuses on daily living skills, sensory integration and fine motor skills.

Ocular

Pertaining to the eye.

Ocular Dominance

The tendency of one eye to be used in such activities as sighting a rifle or threading a needle.

Ocular Nystagmus

Bell's term (1808) for the spasmodic rotations of the eyeballs after an individual has been rotated.

Oculomotor Nerve

The third cranial nerve. It mediates the muscles of the eye, except the superior oblique and the external rectus.

Odorimetry

The measurement of the intensity of olfactory sensations.

Olfaction

Sense of smell.

Olfactometer

Apparatus for stimulating the olfactory membrane by a stimulus of controlled intensity. Units of intensity are called olfacties.

Ontogeny

The developmental history of an individual.

Operant Conditioning

A term introduced by the US Psychologist B. Skinner to designate a special way in which conditioned relationships form. Unlike the classic (Pavlov's) way, which Skinner called respondent, in operant conditioning, the animal first makes a certain movement (spontaneous or initiated by experimenter) and then receives a reinforcement.

Operational

Based on empirical and measurable phenomena.

Ophthalmograph

Apparatus for photographing the eye movements in reading.

Ophthalmoplegia

Paralysis of muscles which move the eyeball. Internal ophthalmoplegia is the paralysis of the muscles of the iris and the ciliary body.

Ophthalmoscope

An instrument for looking into eye chamber and examining the fundus oculi.

Ophthalmotonometer

Apparatus for measuring the movements of the eyeballs, as in reading or surveying a scene.

Opthalmoplegic

Pertaining to the paralysis of the ocular muscles.

Opthalmologist

A medical doctor that deals with diagnosis and treatment of defects and conditions of the eye; he performs surgery or prescribes other types of treatment including glasses.

Optacon

Optacon is about the size of a dictionary, weigh eight pounds, and operates on batteries. The user of this device passes a hand held scanner over printed material with one hand and visual letters are converted by pins into tactile letters on the index finger of the other hand.

Optic Agnosia

Inability to recall the correct names of objects seen, as a result of cerebral lesions.

Optic Chiasm

The crossing of the optic nerves just in front of the tubu cinereum.

Optic Disk

The small, round prominence where the optic nerve emerges into the eyeball.

Optic Nerve

The second cranial nerve, connecting the visual center in the occipital lobe and the retina.

Optician

This person can only grind lenses and fit them in frames.

Optometriest

Examines eyes and prescribes corrective lenses. He does not have a medical degree and cannot prescribe medicines or treat eye diseases or disorders.

Oral-Aural Approach

The main focus of this type of approach is to teach the child to use his residual hearing and to speech read.

Oral Method

Method of teaching communication of language to deaf or hard of hearing individuals by spoken words. An individual's use of his remaining senses to establish his position and relationship to objects in his environment.

Organ of Corti

The receptor structure for hearing which contains the dendrites of the auditory nerve. It was described by Corti in 1851.

Organic Hearing Loss

The term organic hearing loss implies to a definite defect in auditory system (that may be in external middle or inner ear or in the auditory nerve) resulting into hearing loss.

Orientation

Awareness of one's true relationship, spatial and temporal, in the environment; Orientation is a learned familiarity with regard to relating to the environment.

Orientation and Mobility Specialist

A certified teacher specializing in teaching the visually impaired to travel safely and efficiently.

Orthopaedically Handicapped Children

Severe orthopaedic impairment which adversely affects a child's educational performance. The term includes impairments caused by congenital anomaly, disease and impairments from other causes.

Orthotics

An orthotics is an appliance which is added to the patient to enable better use of a body part, e.g., dynamic cock-up splint for wrist drop due to radial nerve palsy, knuckle bender splint and opponens splints for median nerve palsy. Spinal orthoses are used in spinal injury and tuberculosis of the spine; Cervical collar is used in cervical spondylosis and cervical injury.

Ossicles

The bones of the middle ear, namely malleus, incus and stapes. These are joined to one another and form a chain. This chain of ossicles is suspended in the air filled middle ear cavity. It connects the tympanic membrane to the inner ear.

Osteomyelitis

Inflammation of the marrow of the bone.

Other Health Impaired

Limited strength, vitality or alertness due to chronic or acute health problems such as a heart condition, tuberculosis, rheumatic, fever nephritis, asthma, sickle, cell anemia, hemophilia, epilepsy lead poisoning, leukemia, or diabetes which adversely affects a child's educational performance.

Otitis Media

It is an inflammation or infection of the middle ear.

Otolaryngologist

An ear, nose and throat doctor.

Otology

The study and treatment of the ear.

Otosclerosis

Otosclerosis is a hereditary disease that is more common in females than in male. The disease begins at a young age. This is a disease process that affects the bony capsule of the inner ear, turning the normally hard bone into spongy bone.

Overt

Open to objective observation.

Oxycephaly

Distortion of the skull giving the head a steeple-shaped appearance; acrocephaly.

P

Palsy

Paralysis.

Panic

A condition of fear or anxiety together with a disorganization of behaviour.

Papilledema

Edema or swelling of the optic nerve.

Para

Greek prefix meaning "beyond" "distortation or perversion of".

Paracusia

Distorted sense of hearing.

Paralanguage

Refers to the non-verbal elements of communication used to modify meaning and convey emotion. It may be expressed consciously or unconsciously and it include pitch, volume and intonation of speech, sometimes, the definition is restricted to vocally produced sounds.

Paralysis

Complete or partial loss of feeling or movement; Loss of power to move (the whole body or a part may be involved) or an impowerment of power to move.

Paralysis Agitans

Shaking palsy; Parkinson's disease.

Paramimia

Inability to correctly imitate gestures.

Paraplegia

Paralysis of the legs and lower part of the body; Paralysis involving only legs. Paralysis of the lower half of the body.

Paraprofessional

Non-professional person trained to assist professionals in their work.

Parasympathetic Nervous System

The cranial and the sacral portions of the autonomic nervous system.

Parathyroid Glands

Small endocrine glands located near the thyroid.

Parietal Lobe

The lobe of the cerebrum lying above the fissure of sylvius.

Partially Sighted

Individuals have sufficient vision to read print; One whose visual acuity is better than 20/200.

Pathogenic

Causing disease or disorder.

Pathology

The study of the nature of disease and its resulting structural and functional changes.

Pathological

Abnormal, diseased or disorder.

Path Sounder

This is used in conjunction with a cane and reaches ahead of the blind traveler several steps beyond the reach of the cane to provide information about possible obstacles.

Pediatrics

The study and treatment of children and their care.

Peer Group

Age mates who provide a supportive social network for a person, especially an adolescent.

Pellagra

Physical disorder due to lack of nicotinic acid.

Perinatal

The period of time at or immediately after birth.

Perception

The ability of a person to organize integrate sensory information in a meaningful way; Awareness of sensory stimulation; Recognition of a quality without distinguishing meaning which is the result of a complex set of reactions including sensory stimulation, organization within nervous system, and memory.

Perceptual-motor

A term describing the interaction of various channels of perception with motor activity. The channels of perception include visual, auditory, tactual and kinesthetic.

Performance Test

Non-verbal psychological test; A non-verbal measure of intelligence, usually in the form of blocks which are to be fitted into recessions. Seguin (1842) developed one of the first test of this type (The Seguin form board).

Peripheral Nervous System

The nerves which join the brain and the cord with the receptors and the effectors.

Peripheral Vision

What the person sees outsides of their field of vision by moving their eyes, not their head; Indirect vision, or that which is mediated by other areas of the retina than the forea. It was first described by Young (1801) and Purkinje (1825) was the first to describe the differential sensitivity to colours in various peripheral areas of vision.

Perservation

The tendency for one to persist in a specific act or behaviour after it is no longer appropriate.

Personality

Personality is the integrated and dynamic organization of the physical, mental, moral and social qualities of the individual as that manifests itself to others in social life; According to G.W. Allport, personality is the dynamic organization within the individual of those psychophysical systems that determine his unique adjustments to his environment; Personality is that which permits a prediction of what a person will do in a given situation (R.B. Catell).

Personality Disorder

A non-psychotic illness characterized by enduring patterns of perceiving, relating to and thinking about oneself and the environment in ways that are maladaptive. The individual uses inflexible behaviour patterns to fulfil his or her own needs and attain self-satisfaction, often at the expense of others and society in general. Results in significant functional impairment and/or subjective distress.

Pervasive Developmental Delay

Not otherwise specified (PDD-NOS).

Basically a diagnosis of developmental, delays that could be on the autism spectrum.

Petit Mal

Convulsive disorder characterized by brief losses of consciousness.

Petit Mal Seizure

A mild form of epilepsy with momentary lapse of consciousness.

Phenometer

Apparatus for measuring auditory acuity (Wundt, 1893)

Phenotype

Any observable morphological, physical, or behavioural feature of an organism; Lewin's term (1927) for similarities in the behaviour of a number of individuals. It is to be distinguished from a genotype, which is the cause for the behaviour and which, therefore, differs from individual to individual, though outward behaviour may be similar.

Phenylketoneuria (PKU)

Disturbance of portion metabolism frequently associated with mental retardation; It is an error in metabolism that causes affected individuals to be unable to use the essential amino acid, phenylalamine (which is found in high protein foods), whose consequent build-up causes brain damage and profound intellectual disability.

Phobia

An irrational fear of something; Pathological fear of some specific stimulus or situation.

Phoneme

Basic unit of sound by which the more complex parts of language (morphemes, like words or sentences) are formed.

Phonetic Method

An approach to the treatment of articulation difficulties in which the therapist directs attention to the specific movements and placements of the articulatory structures.

Phonics

The study of speech sounds with special reference to reading.

Phonology

The study of how speech sounds (Phonemes) join to make words.

Photophobia

Sensitivity to light.

Phrenology

The pseudo-science which determines mental status by the protrusions and recessions on the skull.

Physical Therapy

Helps overcome neuromuscular disability through exercise, massage, heat, water, light and electricity.

Physical Therapist

Provides evaluation and treatment of physical disabilities to help the person improve the use of bones, muscles, joints and nerves through exercise and massage.

Placement

The program that the team of specialists and parent decide is the most appropriate for the student.

Plexus

An intricate network of nerve fibers lying outside the central nervous system.

Plus Curriculum

The plus curriculum is not something extra, it is compensatory. It contains skills and competencies which, if developed early, result in the leaning of the general curriculum meant for sighted children. The special areas of plus curriculum area – Braille, Orientation and mobility, Daily living skills, sensory training, social skills, use of equipments like braillers and Abacus.

Pinna

The auricle or outer portion of the ear.

Pitch

The attribute of auditory sensations whereby they are judged to be relatively high, middle or low; This is the psychological attribute of intensity. Higher the frequency, higher in the perceived pitch; Highness or lowness of a tone or a sound.

Pituitary

An endocrine gland in the base of the brain; Dwarfism, Acromegaly, and gigantism are associated with pituitary dysfunction.

Poliomyelitis

Poliomyelitis is an acute infective disease, caused by the Poliovirus. Humans are the sole natural reservoir for poliovirus. Poliovirus enters the human body through the mouth and elementary tract. The virus multiples in the intestines. It then travels to the regional lymph nodes and reticulo endothelial structures. Poliovirus selectively damages some special areas in the nervous system. Poliomyelitis occurs mostly in young children. The clinical picture ranges from inapparent illness to extensive paralysis of the muscles, respiratory failure and even death.

Polydactylism

Supernumerary fingers and/or toes.

Polygenic

Involving a combination of hereditary influences.

Positive Reinforcement

Any stimulus which, when made contingent upon a particular response, will strengthen that response. The acid test of which stimuli are positively reinforcing to a given individual is whether or not it does strengthen a given response.

Posterior (Dorsal)
Back of the body.

Post-Lingual Hearing Loss
The term post-lingual hearing loss suggests that hearing loss developed after the language had developed significantly.

Post Natal
Period of time after birth.

Posture
Posture is a motor action in which muscles act for keeping the entire body in a given alignment. This provides formation of an essential body-base and maintains stability of the body. There is no movement of the entire body or its part/parts. There are two basic types of postures: Inactive and Active postures.

Pragmatics
The functional use of language in social contexts.

Pre-academic Skills
Skills that are needed before formal academic instruction begins, (for example, ability to identify letters, sounds, shapes, colours, numbers).

Prelingual Hearing Loss
The hearing loss developed prior to the language learning age.

Pre-natal
Period of time before birth.

Presbycusis
A sensorineural loss caused due to degenerative changes of aging.

Preservation
Repeating an activity to an extreme that it interferes with other activities.

Presbyopia

A condition of inelasticity of the lens which occurs in later maturity and which is difficult to see near objects clearly.

Prevalence

The term prevalence refers specially to all current cases (old & new) existing at a given point of time or over a period of time in a given population.

Presenile Psychosis

Alzheimer's or Pick's disease, or premature deterioration of the brain.

Primary Dementia

Kraepelin's term (1883) for a major category of mental disorders occurring in adolescence and differentiated from other disorders by a withdrawal from reality, fantasies, and inappropriate emotional behaviour.

Primary Reinforcer

Those stimuli that can strengthen behaviours they follow without prior learning. These reinforcing stimuli derive their reinforcing power from the fact that they satisfy physiological needs of the organism (e.g. food, water).

Process Oriental Methods

Those methods emphasizing the processes of language, such as decoding encoding and memory; distinguished from task-oriented methods.

Prognosis

Predicted outcome of a disorder'; Judgment concerning the course, duration, termination and recovery from a pathological condition.

Progressive Hearing Loss

This term indicates that hearing loss is getting worse with time. This may be due to any infection or hereditary disorder.

Proprioceptive Receptors

Proprioceptive receptors are located in our muscles and joints. These receptors allow children to know where their body is in space and to perform tasks automatically without looking.

Prosencephalon

The forebrain, which includes, in addition to the cerebral hemisphere, the following: optic bulb tracts, tube cinereum corpora mamillaria, and the posterior perforated spot.

Prosody

Comprising rate, intonation and volume.

Prosthesis

Artificial device that replaces a missing body part; Prosthesis can be for external or internal use. Internal prosthesis are the joint replacements, heart valves etc. External prosthesis are used for upper and lower limbs which have been amputated, for example, Jaipur foot, Cosmetic hand.

Protanopia

Real blindness.

Proximal

Nearer to trunk (example, shoulder is proximal to elbow).

Psyche

The mind.

Psychologist

A specialist in the field of psychology.

Psychometrician

A psychologist who administers batteries of tests.

Psychomotor

Motor behaviour associated with psychological processes. Psychomotor tests are tests of motor skill which depend upon sensory or perceptional motor co-ordination.

Psychomotor Agitation

Agitated motor activity.

Psychomotor Seizure

Convulsive disorder characterized by a wide range of behaviour disturbances of a dissociative seizure.

Psycholinguistics

It is the fusion of two independent but related fields of Psychology and Linguistics. Its primary concern is to explain the psychological or mental processes that takes place in an individual when one is engaged in the act of communication.

Psychomotor Retardation

A generalized slowing of psychologic and physical activity, frequently occurring as a symptom of severe depression.

Psychosis

A profound (acute or chronic) mental disorder manifesting itself in distorted reflection of reality, clouded consciousness, changed self-awareness and behaviour, and changed attitude towards the environment; Person has difficulty differentiating between fantasy and reality.

Psychosomatic

Pertaining to both mind and body.

Punishment

A process of weakening behaviour which can take one of two forms. First, an aversive or noxious stimulus can be made contingent on the response to be weakened, second, a positively reinforcing stimulus can be withheld or removed contingent on the response to be weakened.

Pure Tones

These are that sounds that contain only one frequency. Its wave form repeats itself every 't' seconds.

PWD Act (Persons with Disabilities Act, 1995)

The legislation called Persons with Disabilities Act (PWD Act) was enacted in 1995 and came into form with effect from 1996. This Act sets the stage to protect the rights of persons with disabilities to provide equal educational opportunities and full participation.

Q

Quadriplegia

Paralysis of all four limbs of the body.

Questionnaire

A method of collecting primary sociological and socio-psychological information through verbal communication.

Quotient Intelligence

Mental age divided by chronological age (usually multiplied by 100 to clear of decimals).

R

Range of Motion

The amount of person is able to move their joints and limbs.

Rapport

A relationship of ease, harmony, and accord between the subject and examiner or therapist.

Rating Scale

A technique that allows to classify the totality of objects under study by the prominence of their common property.

Reaction Time

The interval between stimulus and response.

Readability Level

An indication of the difficulty of reading material in terms of the grade level at which it might be expected to be read successfully.

Readiness Test

A test that measures the extent to which an individual has achieved a degree of maturity or acquired certain skills or information needed for undertaking successfully some new learning activity. Thus, a reading readiness test indicates the extent to which a child has reached a developmental stage where he may profitably begin a formal instructional program in reading.

Re-auditorization

The ability to understand and recognize words so that they can be remembered and recalled for latter use.

Recall

The revival of a past experience.

Receptive Language

Language that is spoken or written by others and received by the individual. The receptive language skills are listening and reading; The understanding of spoken and written communication as well as gestures.

Receptive Language Disability

Inability to understand spoken language.

Receptor

The ending of the sensory nerve which is stimulated by some form of energy. (The receptor is the dendrite of an afferent nerve cell).

Recognition

The feeling of familiarity when a previously encountered situation is present.

Redgreen Blindness

Dichromatism.

Reflex

A movement performed involuntarily as a result of the stimulation of a sensory nerve which sends impulse through a connecting nerve to a nerve center and thence to a motor nerve; this functional unit of the nervous system is called a reflex arc.

Refractive Errors

Refractive errors is defined as "a defect in the eye that prevents light rays from being brought to a single focus exactly on the retina (Bourgeault, 1969)".

Regression

The return to a previous or earlier developmental phase of adaptation partially or symbolically of more infantile ways of gratification. Most clearly seen in psychoses.

Rehabilitation

Rehabilitation is the process of the handicapped to achieve the fullest physical, mental, vocational, economic and social usefulness of which they are capable; Rehabilitation procedure is an attempt to reduce the effect of their disability, more through a process of exploration, understanding and action; James Drever (1953) defines 'rehabilitation' as restoring a lost ability or abilities to a satisfactory conditions after these abilities have been impaired, usually through injury.

Reinforcement

Rewarding a desired response in operant conditioning; following the conditioned stimulus with the unconditioned stimulus in classical conditioning; A procedure to strengthen or weaken a response by the administration of immediate rewards (positive reinforcement) or punishment (negative reinforcement).

Reinforcer

Anything that increases the strength of a behaviour; Any stimulus event that can be used to strengthen a behaviour it follows.

Rejection

Deprivation of affection.

Relapse

The return of a disorder shortly after the period of convalescence or readjustment.

Related Services

Other support services that a child with disabilities requires such as transportation, occupational, physical and speech pathology services, interpreters and medical services etc.

Relaxation Therapy

E. Jacobson's technique of progressive relaxation (1929), which consists of teaching patients how to relax skeletal muscles and the incipient motor responses found in essential hypertension, the anxieties, stuttering, insomnia, and the like.

Reliability

The accuracy and repeatability of a measurement.

Relief Copy Machine

This machine instantly produces relief of writing both in print and in handwriting. This machine consists of a dry-type standard copying machine and a foaming unit. Lines, dots, figures, illustrations, graphs, maps, patterns, letters and photographs are first copied on relief copy paper. The foaming unit then applies thermal treatment so that dark plates will emerge as relief. It will require about ten seconds to produce a relief copy.

Remediation

Methods of instruction to correct deficits of student performance.

Remembering

The activity of reviving memory images.

Residential School

This school provides a "home away – from home" setting for the child and is primarily used for a child who is multi-handicapped or whose school district cannot give him the special help he needs.

Residual Hearing

The amount of hearing that is left after a person has a hearing loss.

Resource Room

A room that serves the children's needs to learn, specific skills within the least restrictive environment.

Resource Teacher

A specialist who works with children with special learning needs and acts as a consultant to other teachers, providing materials and methods to help children who are having difficulty within the regular classroom. The resource teacher may work from a centralized resource room within a school where appropriate materials are housed.

Response

An overt action resulting from a stimulus.

Retardation

A slight degree of mental deficiency.

Retina

The innermost membrane of the eyeball which contains the rods and the cones. Kolliver (1854) was one of the first to describe the histology of the retina.

Retinal Rivalry

Helmholtz's term (1863) for the simultaneous stimulation of the retinas by two different colours or by designs which cannot be fused. The impression is unstable and fluctuating.

Rett Syndrome

It occurs only in girls and is characterized by normal early development followed by decelerated developmental progress and head growth Children with this progressive condition have seizures, develop hyperventilation, lose purposeful hand movement and develop instead wringing of hands, develop spasticity and often lose the ability to walk independently (Shonkoff & Marshall 2000).

Reward

The incentive used to motivate animal and human subjects in experiments on learning. It is used in studies of improvement of human efficiency.

Rh Incompatibility

Two different blood groups, of mother and baby (foetus) which are not acceptable because of basic differences.

Rhinencephalon

The olfactory lobe of the brain.

Rhinolalia

A nasal voice.

Rigidity

A tendency for the muscles to become very stiff after they have been extended.

Rods

A receptor for vision, located in the retina. They were first differentiated by Kolliver (1854) and the theory that they respond to light waves giving rise to achromatic sensations was stated by Von Kries. Rods contain visual purple, which is believed to be essential for dark adaptation.

Role Playing

In psychotherapy, a technique which requires the individual to enact a social role other than his own or to try out new roles for himself.

Rubella (German Measles)

A serious viral disease which if it occurs during the first trimester of pregnancy, is likely to cause a deformity in the foetus.

S

Saccule (Sacculus)

A membranous sac in the inner ear (which together with utricle) is thought to contain receptors for static equilibrium.

Scala Media (Cochlear Duct)

The smallest of the three membranous sacs in the inner ear. It is filled with endolymph, and it contains the organ of corti.

Scala Tympani

A membranous sac in the inner ear which communicates with the scale vestibuli at the belicotrema. It is filled with perilymph.

Scale

An instrument for measuring permanent properties of an object, consisting of a numerical system in which relations between various properties of objects are expressed by the properties of numerical series. Initially, four types of numerical systems were distinguished to determine four respective levels (or scales) of measurement, namely, the nominal scale, the ordinal scale, the interval scale and the proportional scale.

Schemograph

Apparatus for tracing the outlines of the visual field.

Schizoneurosis

A psychopathological syndrome on the borderline of psychoneurosis and schizophrenice (Psychosis).

School Psychologist

Person who is a consultant to teachers counselors and administrators who gives diagnostic tests to students.

Sclera

The outermost covering of the eyeball. The sclerotic coat is tough and opaque. The cornea is continuous with the sclera and covers about 1/6th of the surface, the sclera including the remaining five-sixths.

Sclerosis

Hardening of nervous tissues, or a thickening of the walls of the arteries. In multiple sclerosis, the hardening process occurs in various parts of the nervous system; and the principal symptoms are as follows: nystagmus, weakness, slurred or monotonous talk, spastic gait, and intention tremors.

Scotoma

A dark spot in the visual field, usually due to a lesion in the retina. Scotoma may be sensed as a ring around the macula lutea flashes of light sparks, dimness and total absence of visual sensitivity in a certain part of the field. Their location and extent are mapped by scotometer.

Scotopic Adaptation

Darkness adaptation (Aubert 1865).

Screening

A brief process designed to identify individuals with an increased risk of having disorders that warrant immediate attention, intervention or more comprehensive review. Screening is not intended to provide an accurate diagnosis, but to distinguish those individuals who are particularly troubled and may need a more comprehensive evaluation in order to identify specific deficits.

Seizure

A temporary burst of abnormal electrical activity in the brain. The brain loses control over muscles, consciousness, senses and thoughts.

Self-Care Skills/Self-Help Skills/Daily Living Skills

The ability to care for oneself, usually refers to basic habits of dressing, eating etc.

Self-Concept

A relatively stable and more or less conscious phenomenon, emotionally experienced as a unique system of the individual's ideas about himself, basing on which he interacts with other people and develops an attitude towards himself; self concept is an integral image of one's self albeit not devoid of inner contradictions.

Self-Consciousness (Technically)

The awareness of one's own identity as a more or less persisting entity.

Self-Contained

A classroom is self-contained if the students in it spend the entire day with the same teacher. Elementary education is almost always conducted in self-contained classrooms.

Self-Contained Class

A classroom specifically for special education students.

Self-Esteem

A feeling about one's self-worth or self-concept; It is a judgement about whether our abilities and qualities meet or fall short of the standards were believe are idea. In other words, self-esteem is a comparison between the self-concept and ideal self (Burns 1982).

Sementic Aphasia

Head's term (1920) for loss of ability to understand the meaning of words, a condition which results from an organic pathology in the brain.

Semicircular Canals

Three osseous canals, containing membranous sacs, lying at right angles to one another in the inner ear. They are named as follows – Anterior or superior canal; Posterior or vertical canal; and lateral or horizontal canal. The enlargement of each canal as it leaves the vestibule is called ampulla. They mediate the sense of equilibrium (Flourens 1824) or the static sense (a concept introduced by J. Bruner 1875).

Senile

Pertaining to old age.

Sensation

The state of awareness which results when a sense organ is stimulated and which cannot be analyzed into any elements.

Sense Experience

Awareness which results from direct stimulation of sense organs.

Sense Organ

The receptor and the accessory apparatus considered as one (e.g. the eye or the ear).

Sense Perception

Immediate interpretation or recognition of data present to sense.

Sensitivity

Responsiveness to stimulation.

Sensory Acuity

Threshold of responsiveness to various stimuli.

Sensory Integration

Permits the use of two hands as a team, planning of movement and accurate positioning of hands, all of which are essential to children's fine motor skills (Exner 1989).

Sensory Nerve

A nerve fiber which connects a receptor to the brain or the spinal cord.

Sensory Neural Hearing Loss

A hearing impairment that is usually permanent results when the inner ear or nerves which carry the sound waves to the brain are damaged.

Sensory Skills

These include seeing, hearing, smelling, touching and tasting all the ways that we take-in information about the word around us.

Sentiments

A principle and relatively stable form of attitudinal response towards objects and phenomena.

Serious Emotional Disturbance (SED)

A student may be identified as SED for not having satisfactory inter-personal relationship with peers and teachers or for displaying "inappropriate types of behaviour or feelings".

Serotonium

Chemical mediator in the transmission of the nerve impulse; neuroharmone.

Set

A temporary condition which favours the selection of certain stimuli or facilitates a particular type of response.

Severely Mentally Retarded

The general IQ of 20 to 34 those who fall between the profoundly retarded and moderately retarded.

Shaping

A procedure for developing new, or more complex, behaviour through the reinforcement of successive approximations to the goal behaviour. This procedure uses both positive reinforcement and extinction procedures to develop these closer approximations.

Sheltered Workshop

A facility which provides occupational training and/or protective employment of handicapped persons.

Sibling

Brother or sister born of the same parents.

Sibling Rivalry

Rivalry between brothers and sisters.

Signed English

Sign language that follows English Syntax and Grammar.

Sign Language

Using gestures instead of spoken words to communicate; A system of communication among the deaf through conventional hand or body movements which represents ideas, objects, action etc.; Sign language differ from country to country and also within each country to some extent.

Sinistrality

Left-handedness.

Situation

A complex pattern of stimuli, every factor which determines the behaviour of an individual at any given moment.

Skeletal Musculature

The striated (striped) muscle fibres attached to the bones and controlled by the central nervous system.

Smooth Muscle

Unstriated muscle fibre controlled by the autonomic system.

Social Intelligence

Ability to deal with, and adjust to, other persons. Traits considered to be measurable aspects of social intelligence are the following; sense of humour, memory for names and faces, common sense in social relations, recognition of the mental state of the speaker and common observation of social behaviour.

Socio-linguistics

Socio-linguistics includes the study of structure and use of language that relates to its social and cultural functions.

Socialization

Acquiring the cultural values, knowledge and skills which allow one to function productively in a society; Shaping of individual characteristics and behaviour through the stimuli and reinforcement provides.

Software Automatic Mouth (SAM)

SAM is an all software speech synthesizer for the Apple and Atari micro computers. The disk is capable of producing speech, and an unlimited vocabulary and fully adjustable pitch and rate.

Somnabulism

The tendency towards muscular twitching, spasms, or convulsions from even slight mechanical or electrical stimulation.

Somatic

Pertaining to the body.

Somatic Nervous System

The part of the peripheral nervous system that carries messages from the senses to the central nervous system and between the central nervous system and the skeletal muscles.

Somatogenic Disorder

One which has an organic etiology.

Sonic Guide

This device contains ultrasonic sensors mounted in a pair of glasses, with non-occluding ear moulds to obtain signals reflected from objects within its field. Differences in sound provide the wearer with information on distance, direction and surface characteristic of the object.

Spasm

Sudden contraction of muscle or group of muscles.

Spastic Movements

Those characterized by sudden, intense, contractions of muscles.

Spasticity

Tense contracted muscles usually seen in people with cerebral palsy.

Special Class in Regular School

A student receives his academic instruction from a special education teacher, but may attend school wide activities such as assemblies, concerts or non-academic classes such as physical education or industrial art with his peers.

Special Day Schools

Schools designed for students who have a serious handicap or are multiply handicapped and need comprehensive special education services for their entire school day.

Special Education

It refers to education of children with special needs in all settings, including special schools integrated and inclusive settings or non-formal education. It is special only in so far as support services are provided. It is based on the assumption that education of children with special needs calls for support services in all settings in terms of special technology or resource support; One who has special training or preparation for teaching the handicapped, may also work co-operatively with the regular classroom teacher by sharing unique skills and competencies.

Special Education Programs/Services

Programs and services for children over 3 years old with special needs at no cost to families.

Special Needs

A child who has disabilities or who is at risk of developing disabilities that may require special education services.

Speech Center

Usually denoting Broca's area (1861).

Speech Disorders

According to the White House Conference data (1931), the following (in order of frequency): oral inactivity, structural disorders in articulations; stuttering; sound substitution; functional disorders of the voice; Dialectal, structural disorders of the voice; Articulatory disorders resulting from paralysis; aphasia; hard of hearing and speech; and disorders of the voice resulting from paralysis.

Speech Impaired

Communication disorder such as stuttering, impaired articulation, a language impairment, or a voice impairment, which adversely affects a child's educational performance.

Speech Pathology

The study and treatment of all aspects of functional and organic speech defects and disorders after the same as speech correction.

Speech Pathologist/Speech Therapist

A person qualified who improves and/or correct communication problems; The work of speech therapist/pathologist divides into two principal categories: Alleviating speech disorders and organizing and administering the speech correction programme.

Speech Reading

Same as Lip reading.

Speech Trainer

A speech trainer can be considered as a large size hearing aid. It is a kind of master hearing aid which can be used for different types of hearing losses. There are two types of Speech Trainers – monotype and stereotype.

Sphygmomanometer

Apparatus for measuring blood-pressure, as in studies of the physiology of emotion (Marston 1917).

Splinter Skill

A skill which is not an integral part of the orderly sequential development. It is a skill mastered (usually under pressure) ahead of the usual developmental sequence or a child with poor overall motor co-ordination may be able to skip rope expertly. Rope skipping is in that case a splinter skill.

Spina Bifida

Child is born with an open vertebrae in the spinal column; In this congenital paralytic condition there is lack of closure of the bony elements of the vertebral column with possible protrusion of nerves. Spina Bifida maya lead to loss of voluntary control of the lower extremities, either total or partial and some loss of sensation.

Spinal Chord

The long, cylindrical column in the vertical cord. The principal ascending fibers are the following: Spinothalmic, column of Goll; column of Burdach; direct cerebellar tract; and the tract of Gowers.

Spinal Nerves

(In Man) The thirty-one pairs of nerves attached to the spinal cord and named (from the area of emergence) as follows: Cervical (8); thoracic (12); lumbar (5); Sacral (5); and Coccygeal (1). Charles Bell (1807) discovered that the anterior nerve roots of the spinal cord are motor; the posterior nerve roots, sensory.

Staffing

An interdisciplinary conference bringing together several professional experts, each of whom has examined a given patient for the purpose of combining diagnostic knowledge in order to arrive at a decision concerning the nature, the initiation, or the continuation of treatment.

Standard Deviation

A statistical measure of variability from the mean; It is the square root of the mean of the sum of squares of the deviations from the mean. It is a popular measure of spread of scores in a distribution.

Standardized Test

A test taken by many students under identical conditions which allows results to be compared statistically to a standard such as a norm or criteria.

Stanford Revision of the Binet-Simen Tests

An individual test of intelligence which Terman and Associates developed (1916) from the Binet Simen Scales (1905, 1908, 1911). It contains ninety items (36 more than Binet Simen), and it was standardized on about 2,300 subjects. In 1937, Terman Merill, and associates published another vision. Two scores are obtained from their revisions' mental age and intelligence quotient.

Stapedectomy

The surgical procedure used for otosclerosis to restore hearing is called stapedectomy.

Stapes

This is an stirrup shaped bone. This is a smallest bone not only in the middle ear but also in the whole body. This bone measures only 2.5 mg in weight and less than half the length of malleus and incus.

Statistics

The word statistics is derived from Latin word "status" which means political condition or status. Hence, the method of enumeration by which a state or condition is known as called Statistics; Statistics is the science of estimates and probabilities (Boddington); Statistics is the science which deals with the collection, classification and tabulation of numerical facts as the basis for explanation, description and comparison of phenomena (Louitt).

Stereotype

Purposeless repetition of words and/or actions, as in catatonia.

Stereotyping

A biased generalization, usually about a social or national group in which individuals are falsely assigned traits they do not possess.

Stimulus

Any form of energy which elicits a response.

Strabismus

Cross eyed-ness.

Striped Muscles

The skeletal muscles, which under microscopic examinations are observed to have a striated or striped, appearance and which are involved in adjustments to the external environment.

Stroke

Stroke is characterized by sudden loss of motor control usually hemiplegia, i.e., involvement of face, arm and leg of one side. It may be accompanied by unconsciousness, speech disturbance, visual and hearing loss, numbers, burning pain, sensory deficient and psychiatric disturbances.

Strong Vocational Interest Blank

420 items to be marked like indifferent, dislike, which when scored according to weight established for various occupations discover whether a person's interests resemble those of given occupational group (Strong 1927). It has been extensively used in reasoning studies and in counselling.

Stuttering

Deviation in the fluency of speech; A disorganization in the rhythm of speech accompanied by tonic spasm of the larynx abdominal expiration and thoracic inspiration, tremors, prolongation of certain sounds and repetition of other sounds (includes stammering); Disturbance in the fluency of speech. It is observed as sudden blushing or growing pale as pharyngeal spasms. It is manifestation of the transformation of very strong somato psychic tension of spastic symptoms.

Successive Approximation

The procedure used in shaping a behaviour. The subject is reinforced for successfully closer approximations to the desired behaviour until that behaviour is emitted.

Symbol

Any stimulus (e.g. Object, spoken word, ideational element) which elicits a response originally attached to another stimulus.

Sympathicotonia

A state resulting from high tension in the sympathetic nervous system manifested by accelerated pulse, high blood pressure, dilated pupils or hypo acidity of the stomach.

Sympathetic Nervous System

The Theracicolumbar portion of the autonomic nervous system, which consists of a paired chain of ganglia and efferent fibers innervating the visceral organs, duct and ductless glands, muscle walls of blood vessels and so on.

Symptom

A manifestation of disordered functioning, including both physical and psychological aspects.

Synapse

The functional junction of the axon and the dendrite of nerve cells.

Synchronous

Communication in which interaction between participants is simultaneous.

Syndactylism

Web fingers or toes.

Syndrome

A pattern of symptoms indicating a given disorder; a complex of symptoms; a set of symptoms which occur together.

Syntax

The order of words in sentences; The grammar system of a language. The linguistic rules of word order and the function of words in a sentence.

Syphilis

A venereal disease caused by spirochoeta pallida.

Systole

The contraction of the heart.

T

Taccom

Taccom is a cigarette package size device that can be carried around in person's pocket. It is essentially a radio receiver, stimulated by a signal from a small transmitter at the point under "surveillance" that produces vibrations and thereby provides an adequate tactile warning to the individual. This equipment is mostly used by deaf-blind persons.

Tachy

Greek word meaning "rapid".

Tactile

Pertaining to the sense of touch. Touch is a popular term for the four cutaneous sensations; Pressure, cold, warmth, pain.

Tactile Aids

Tactile aids are an effective transmitters of acoustic information and have proven to be helpful for deaf adults in day to day use. Tactile aids need to be supplemented with lip reading for better speech perception.

Tactile Defensiveness

Child over reads or avoids any kind of touch.

Tactile (Touch) Receptions

They are located in skin. The touch system is the first part of the nervous system to begin functioning in utero and is the most mature of the sensory systems at birth. The skin sends the most sensory information to the brain. It comprises two sub-systems; the protective system that warns the danger (the flight or fight response) and the discriminative system that gives information about the properties of objects so that children can recognize objects they feel.

Talent

Unusual proficiency in some field such as music, creative writing or art.

Talipes

Deformed or club foot.

Talking Calculators

This equipment is handy for learning mathematics. The invention of talking calculator is a big breakthrough in the education of visually impaired children. In the talking calculator, numerical entries are read aloud to the student through the earplug.

Tapping Test Knox's

A measure of attention or memory span in which four cubes are touched in various orders of difficulty (e.g. 1-4-3-2, 1-3,2,4), the test was developed by H.A. Knox as a non-language test for use at Ellis Island.

Task Analysis

Breaking down complex skills into highly structural, series of simpler, smaller, sequential sub-skills; The technique of carefully examining a particular task to discover the elements it comprises and the processes required to perform it.

Taste

The sense of gustation. Taste receptors have been called chemoreceptors.

Tay-Sach's Disease
Hereditary disorder of fat metabolism; may be associated with mental retardation.

Techtorial Membrane
The thick membrane which overlies the organ of corti (in the inner ear).

Telecommunication Device for the Deaf (TDD)
Enables those that are deaf to make and receive telephone calls by typing information over the telephone lines.

Teleconferencing
Two way electronic communication between two or more groups in separate location via audio, video and computer systems.

Temporal Lobe
The portion of the cerebral hemisphere which lies below the fissure of sylvius and in front of the exoccipital fissures.

Tenon's Capsule
The socket within which the eyeball is set. It is named for Jacques Rene Tenon (1724-1816) French anatomist.

Termor
Consistent and uncontrolled movements usually seen in people with cerebral palsy.

Teratogens
A teratogen may be defined as an agent or factor which can cause abnormalities of form and function in an exposed foetus. These agents can be infecting agents, chemical actions, nutritional, mechanical.

Testing
Testing is one element of educational assessment and involves eliciting children's responses to questions under structured conditions (McLuughin and Lewis 2001).

Tetanus

A disease causing convulsive seizures, muscular spasms and heightening reflexes.

Thalamus

Lower brain structure serving as a sensory relay center; The ovoid mass at the base of the cerebrum.

Therapy

Treatment; The science which deals with the treatment or application of remedies for the cure, alleviation or prevention of disorder.

Thinking

The process of an individual's cognitive activity, characterized by a generalized and mediated reflection of reality.

Thrombosis

Blood clotting.

Thymas Gland

An endocrine gland lying in the upper part of the thorax and the throat which gradually atrophies about the time of puberty.

Thyroidinism

See cretinism.

Thyroid Glands

Pair of endocrine glands on each side of the neck below the larynx; An endocrine named from its fancied resemblance to a shield (Greek) which lie anterior to the trachea.

Thyroxine

Thyroid gland hormone; Iodine is essential for the production of this hormone.

Timber

This is a psychological dimension corresponding to the

complexity of the sound. This is also referred to as the quality of the sound.

Tinnitus

A noise in the ears, as ringing, buzzing, roaring, clicking etc.

Token Economy

Form of behaviour therapy in which children/individuals earn tokens (reinforcers) for desired behaviour and exchange them for desired items or privileges.

Behaviour modification method in which people are rewarded for appropriate behaviour with tokens that can be exchanged for desired items or privileges.

Tonal Islands

Areas within the field of auditory stimuli which do not elicit a sensation. Inacuities may exist in a limited range of sound waves but the ear may function normally in other ranges.

Tone

Periodic vibration of sound waves evoking an auditory sensation with more or less well defined attributes.

Tone-deafness

Inability to judge differences among the sequential pitches of tones; hence inability to enjoy music.

Tonic Spasm

Sudden, intense contraction of a muscle or group of muscles.

Tonus

Muscular tension, the opposite of tones is flaccidity.

Torticollis

A twisted neck, as in catatonic posture, an organic disorder, or a neurotic pose.

Total Communication

Educating hearing impaired students with a combination of speech and sign language; This method combines all the means and methods – speech, reading, finger spelling, sign language, auditory training etc. The idea is to teach communication to the hearing impaired child by any means. Total communication term was coined by Roy Hol Comb in 1967.

Touch Traffic Lighting System

This system helps the blind or low vision people while crossing the road. A mini-receiver is fixed into the blind person's cane and the signals are felt by him.

Trachoma

This is a form of infection caused by a specific virus which in the chronic form produces severe scarring of the eyelids and cornea.

Tracking

Inappropriate shift in chromosome material.

Tract

A more or less well defined group of tissues, such as columna of the spinal cord or a nerve.

Trainable Mental Retarded (TMR)

A mentally retarded individual who is likely to show distinct physical pathology and form whose training programs are directed primarily at self care rather than vocational development.

Trait

A distinctive pattern of behaviour which is more or less permanent.

Transposition

The exchange of one letter or word for another.

Trauma

Any experience which inflicts serious damage to the organism. It may refer to psychological as well as physiological insult; shock or injury; The term is extended to include mental shocks severe disappointments and tragedies as well as bodily injuries.

Traumatic Experience
One which has a more or less permanent and devastating effect upon one's self-confidence or self esteem.

Tremor
Rhythmic and involuntary muscle movements.

Trimester
Three month period – usually with reference to pregnancy.

Triplegia
Paralysis of the three limbs of the body.

Trisomy
Having three chromosomes instead of the normal pair; seen in Down's syndrome.

Trochlear Nerve
The fourth cranial nerve.

Tuberous Sclerosis
Inherited neo-plastic disease sometimes associated with mental retardation; Epilolia.

Tumor
A mass of tissue having no physiological function but often disrupting the functions of normal tissue.

Tunnel Vision
Restriction of the visual field; The visually impaired person has the feeling of looking through a tunnel; An individual's field of vision is restricted from the usual 180 degrees to 20 degrees.

Twice Special
A student both gifted and handicapped. For example, gifted and learning disabled.

Tympanic Membrane

The drum-like membrane separating the outer from the middle ear.

Tympanoplasty

A surgical process in order to improve hearing through repair or reconstruction of damaged parts of middle ear.

Tyrosine

Amino acid found in protein substances.

U

Ultrasonic

Pertaining to sound waves of higher frequency that can be heard by the human ear.

Unconditional Reflex

An inborn stereotyped response to biologically meaningful environmental effects or changes in the organism's internal medium.

Under-achiever

A child whose school work is not consistent with the teacher's estimate of his or her ability to learn.

Unilateral

Affecting and pertaining to one side. Opposite of bilateral.

Unstraited Muscles

Smooth muscles, often called the involuntary muscles.

Utricle

Membranes sac in the vestibular apparatus of the inner ear.

V

Vagotonia

A state of resulting from high tension in the vagus nerve manifested by slowing down of pulse, arrhythmia, low blood pressure, constricted pupils, peripheral vascular disorders.

Validity

The extent to which a test does the job for which it is used. Validity thus defined has different connotations for various kinds of tests and accordingly, different kinds of validity evidence are appropriate for them. For example: the validity of an achievement test is the extent to which the content of the test represents a balanced and adequate sampling of the outcomes (knowledge skill etc.) of the course or instructional programme, it is intended to cover (content, face or curricular validity).

Vascular

Pertaining to blood vessels.

Versa Braille

Records Braille into tape cassettes and plays them back on the machine reading board.

Versa Braille-II

Converts letters on a personal computer screen into Braille.

Ventral

Forward aspect of an organ or structure; the anterior portion.

Ventricle

Small cavity within the heart or the brain.

Vertigo

Dizziness, A sensation of whirling or dizziness from over stimulation of the semi-circular canal receptors; often associated with disease of the ear and deafness.

Vestibular Apparatus

The portion of the inner ear lying between the cochlea and the semi-circular canals. It contains the utricle and the saccule two membranous sacs filled with liquid. This apparatus contributes to maintenance of posture and balance.

Vicarious Learning

The acquisition of response capabilities without practice. Learning by observation of the behaviour of others (modeling) is an example of vicarious learning.

Video-Conferencing

A tele-conference including two way video.

Visual Acuity

Measured ability to see; How well a person perceives an object or letter from 20 feet.

Visual Discrimination

Ability to detect differences in object, forms, letters or words.

Visual Field

It is referred to the entire area which can be seen without shifting the gaze. Vision in the peripheral area of retina is known as visual field or field of vision.

Visual Handicapped

Visual impairment which, even with correction, adversely affects a child's educational performance. The term includes both partially seeing and blind children.

Visual Impairment

Eyesight which cannot be corrected to normal.

Visual Memory

The ability to remember visual stimuli by significant features on a short and long term basis.

Visual Perception

The identification, organization and interpretation of sensory data received by the individual through the eye.

Visual Specialist

A certified teacher who specializes in meeting the needs of children with visual impairment.

Visual-motor Co-ordination

The ability to co-ordinate vision with the movements of the body or parts of the body.

Viterous Humor

Jelly like substance filling the posterior chamber of the eyeball.

Vocal Abuse

Screaming, yelling or overuse of the vocal folds.

Vocational Guidance

The application of psychological and educational techniques for appraisal of fitness for various occupation, information about occupations, training help him securing a job, and counsel regarding post school training opportunities. The National Vocational Guidance Association was founded in 1915.

Voice Quality

Comprises resonance and breathiness.

Volley Theory of Hearing

View that the neurons discharge at differential rates but synchronously with the sound wave; hence the volley of the impulses reproduces the sound frequency. This theory was propounded by Wever and Bray (1930), American Psychologists, to effect a compromise between the theories of Helmholtz and Rutherford.

Voluntary Control

A controversial, mentalistic term connoting behaviour which is initiated, sustained and terminated by choice. Striated muscles are said to be under direct voluntary control.

Voluntary Movements

External and internal bodily acts consciously regulated by the subject on the basis of his need for reaching the goal represented as the image of anticipated result.

W

WAIS

Wechsler Adult Intelligence Scale.

Walking Aids

Walking Aids are used to increase the mobility of a patient as they enable some of the body weight to be supported by the upper limbs. The different types of walking aids are parallel bars, walking frames, crutches, wheelchairs and sticks etc.

Wave Length

Distance from crest to crest or trough to trough, of light waves.

Wechsler Tests

Series of comprehensive tests of intelligence.

Wernicke's Area

Region in the temporal lobes, a lesion in which is thought to be the etiologic factor in sensory aphasia. Identified by Carl Wernicke (1874).

White Matter

Referring to the whitish appearance of the myelin sheath of medullated nerve fibres. The anatomical difference between grey matter and white matter of nervous tissue was described by Theodor Schwann (1810-1882), a German histologist.

Whole-part Learning

Referring to two procedures for learning. In the whole method, the material is studied in its entirety; In the part method, it is broken up into convenient units for mastery.

WISC

Wechsler Intelligence Scale for Children.

Withdrawal

Process of retreating from society and relationships with others, usually includes lack of interest in social activities and difficulty in communicating with others.

Within Class Regrouping

Students are grouping together within a class for one or more subject areas (usually math and language arts) based on achievement or mastery of the content.

Worry

Undue concern about past behaviour or about anticipated dangers in future behaviour.

Wry Neck (Torticollis)

The defect is due to a contracture of neck muscles drawing the head to the side with the chin pointing in the opposite direction; Neglect to this condition may lead to facial distortion, poor ocular alignment, body imbalance or serious curvature of the spine.

X

Xerophthalmia

(Greek for dry eyes) is a medical condition in which the eye fails to produce tears. It may be caused by a deficiency in vitamin A, and is sometimes used to describe, the lack, although there may be other causes. The treatment depends upon the cause. Artificial tears which lubricate the eye, are the principal symptomatic treatment for dry eye.

XYY Variant

Genetic deviation in which there are two Y (male) chromosomes rather than one, which is more common.

Y

Yellow-blindness

The most uncommon form of colour blindness; A small area (also known as macula flava or macula lutea) which lies in the central posterior section of the retina. The small depression in the "yellow spot" is known as the fovea centralis.

Yoga

(1) Formalized techniques of distract contemplation by Indian philosophers.

(2) System of practices including formalized postures of body, breathing exercises and diets which are said to facilitate self hypnosis and trances.

Z

Zero Reject Concept

This means no child for whatever reason should be rejected from the educational system. The People with Disabilities Act (1995) in India and the legal provisions in many countries (PL 94-142 in USA for instance) in essence advocate that all children must have access to education. If such a 'Zero reject' policy should be achieved children, with profound and multiple disabilities must receive appropriate education.

Zygote

Fertilized Egg.